BLOOD
MOONS

BL👁️👁️D
M👁️👁️NS

DECODING THE IMMINENT HEAVENLY SIGNS

MARK BILTZ

 WND Books

Book designed by Mark Karis

WND Books are distributed to the trade by:
Midpoint Trade Books
27 West 20th Street, Suite 1102
New York, New York 10011
WND Books are available at special discounts for bulk purchases. WND Books, Inc., also publishes books in electronic formats. For more information call (541) 474-1776 or visit www.wndbooks.com.

First Edition
paperback ISBN: 978-1-936488-11-7
eBook ISBN: 978-1-936488-08-7

Library of Congress Catalog-in-Publication Data

Printed in the United States of America
14 15 16 17 18 19 BVG 9 8 7 6 5 4 3 2 1

To Vicki, my fun and beautiful wife of thirty-six years

TABLE OF CONTENTS

FOREWORD BY JOSEPH FARAH   ix

ACKNOWLEDGMENTS   xi

INTRODUCTION   xv

1   MY STORY   1

2   SIGNS & SIGNALS   15

3   SEASONS: SPRING FEASTS   47

4   SEASONS: FALL FEASTS   65

5   GOD'S CALENDAR DAYS AND YEARS   121

6   THE SCIENCE OF THE SIGNS   143

7   FOR THE NAYSAYERS   157

8   THE CONCLUSION OF THE MATTER   165

BIBLIOGRAPHY   174

RESOURCES   176

INDEX   178

FOREWORD BY
JOSEPH FARAH

When I first heard Mark Biltz explain his amazing discovery of a series of lunar and solar eclipses coinciding with important Hebrew calendar dates like Passover and the Feast of Tabernacles over a two-year period, I was intrigued, excited, and fascinated.

That was several years ago, and I made a note to talk with the pastor of El Shaddai Ministries, as we got closer to the critical dates, about the possibility of a book on the significance of his findings. Now, what has become known as the "blood moons phenomenon" is upon us. While others have attempted to place these astronomical events in a proper biblical, prophetic, and historic context, no one is better positioned to do so than Mark Biltz, who has been putting all the pieces together over several years of intense research.

It's not a question of *if* these signs will occur. It's not even a question of *when* they will occur. About that there is no doubt. The only questions that remain to be answered are: what they mean—and whether they are biblical harbingers of things to come for the world and for God's people. No one has perspective on these questions like Mark Biltz. The wisdom of decoding these heavenly messages from our Creator in *Blood Moons* is overwhelmingly persuasive, and I believe this book will, for the first time, answer all the questions curious people of all walks of life will have about the imminent signs in the heavens.

God is trying to get our attention. And I am convinced He has anointed Mark Biltz to help us understand the times in which we live and the urgent warnings God is trying to deliver to us all.

I have not been as enthusiastic about a powerful spiritual teaching since I worked with Rabbi Jonathan Cahn on *The Isaiah 9:10 Judgment,* a documentary movie treatment of his best seller *The Harbinger. Blood Moons* by Mark Biltz is that kind of message—one so detailed, so improbable, so mysterious it could only be the result of divine handiwork.

The Bible says God uses the sun, moon, and stars to communicate with us. Brace yourself and prepare to be shocked by what God is telling us through the heavenly signs.

—*Joseph Farah*

ACKNOWLEDGMENTS

My wife, Vicki Biltz, is the one who lit the fire in me that radically changed both our lives by giving me a book by a Jewish rabbi that opened not only my mind but also the eyes of my heart to a greater understanding of both the *Tanakh* and the New Covenant.

I would like to thank my two sons, Christopher and Andrew, for their encouraging me in getting this book done.

I am indebted to Norm and Sue Belliveau and Bud and Cindy Flowers for the push they gave me in starting El Shaddai Ministries back in 2001. Without them none of this would have ever happened.

I offer special thanks to Dana and Lee Hicks, as they were the ones who were instrumental in launching the Blood Moon teaching worldwide. I was telling them about my finding when they were visiting our El Shaddai booth at the Puyallup Fair in 2008, and Dana said, "This has to get out!" Right there in the booth, he called his friend Bob Ulrich, with *Prophecy in the News*.

I thank Bob, as he allowed me to come on their TV

program with J. R. Church and Gary Stearman. It was *Prophecy in the News* that gave us the TV exposure that we had never had before.

Also coming alongside us was Joseph Farah with WND. His reporting of the amazing discovery on his website launched us into the stratosphere! From there, El Shaddai Ministries doubled in size locally and had to move three times within a year. But more than that, our website has now grown to two hundred thousand live streams or downloads from around the world every month.

I also thank our good friends Bill and Rocio Voiss, who have personally walked beside my wife and me the last few years, encouraging us and so selflessly helping us with our local congregation so I can continue to get the message out. Bill serves as the vice president of El Shaddai Ministries, and without both him and his wife volunteering their help, giving us sound advice, and encouraging us for the last three years, we would not have accomplished all that we have.

I also appreciate my brother Tim, who has incredibly picked up the torch in discovering our family's Jewish roots. He is an avid follower of our website's teachings on the Jewish roots of Christianity. His dogged research of our family genealogy has connected us to our Jewish relatives on our father's side all the way back to the early 1700s. Through his research, we have found our relatives who are listed in Yad Vashem, the Holocaust museum in Israel, as well as our living relatives in France.

I also must acknowledge and thank our local El Shaddai family, without whose consistent support I would not always be motivated to press forward. They are the faithful ones who have stood beside Vicki and me through thick and thin.

Next, I must thank our worldwide live streaming families. So many of you have consistently supported us through your beautiful, encouraging e-mails and by helping us financially to continue our mission to take the Torah to the nations. I have personally enjoyed all the individuals who have taken the time to send me e-mails from Canada, the UK, Australia, Ireland, Japan, the Netherlands, South Africa, India, and the list could go on. People from 192 countries have visited our website, enjoying all the free information, and to all of them Vicki and I say a big THANK YOU!

Last but not least, I want to acknowledge the publishing team for this book. I would like to personally thank Joseph and Elizabeth Farah; Geoffrey Stone, editorial director, who personally helped me edit this work; Renée Chavez, copy editor; Aryana Hendrawan, production editor; Mark Karis, designer; and the marketing team of Michael Thompson and Amanda Prevette. Thank you all!

INTRODUCTION

I n 1975, at age nineteen, I got saved, and for the next
eighteen years, I did as much volunteer work for God as I
could possibly do. But by 1993, when I was thirty-seven
and married with two boys, I had reached a point where
I was totally burned-out on church. Over the years, with
the help of my wife, Vicki, I had volunteered a multitude of
hours working in the children's nursery, doing janitorial work
at the church, and conducting home fellowships for up to
fifty people at our house. Vicki would lead worship; I would
preach and teach, all the while holding down full-time jobs.

In 1994, Vicki was browsing a discount bookstore in
Tacoma, Washington, looking for bird books, when she
saw a book on the significance of the Jewish holy days, by
Rabbi Moshe Braun. She knew how much I loved to read
and felt she just had to get it for me.

That book changed my life. I began to see the incredible
significance of the feasts of the Lord from a whole new perspective. I realized that God had a calendar He went by, and
it definitely wasn't the one I was using! Over the next seven
years, I read everything I could get my hands on that would

help me gain a better understanding of the Bible from this fresh, new point of view. I also found a little congregation that met in Puyallup, Washington, where I was introduced to this new line of thinking.

Then God began to alter my life. I got laid off after nine years from a roofing-manufacturing job in Tacoma, so for the next two years I got back into sales, working first for Brinks Home Security. After a successful year there, I felt God really wanted me to teach what I was learning. So I quit my excellent full-time job and took a part-time job that would allow me more time to focus on starting El Shaddai Ministries. I was blessed to be able to work at the Family Christian Bookstore in Federal Way, Washington. They were very accommodating in my bi-vocational endeavor.

Starting El Shaddai Ministries was life changing for Vicki and me. But in 2008, something radical happened. In March of that year, I saw on the Internet an incredible total lunar eclipse over the Temple Mount in Jerusalem. I had read all the Bible verses in Isaiah, Joel, the Gospels, and Revelation where the text talks about the moon turning to blood and the sun to sackcloth. I began to ponder the possibilities of tying the eclipses mentioned in the Bible to the possible coming of the Messiah.

Because I love science and astronomy, I decided to look into the future occurrences of eclipses. I remembered that NASA has a list of eclipses that covers five thousand years, so I went to the website to see what interesting observations I could find. I noticed that there were four total lunar eclipses in a row for 2014 and 2015. I noted their dates on our calendar.

Vicki and I raised our kids in a small house of about a thousand square feet, so the only "prayer closet" I had was literally the walk-in closet in our bedroom. After visiting NASA's website, I suddenly began waking up around 4 a.m. for several days in a row. Unable to go back to sleep, I would get up and go into the closet to pray for an hour or so.

One morning, as I was praying, a thought popped into my head: *Why don't I compare the dates of the eclipses on the NASA website to the dates on the biblical calendar?* When I did, I was shocked to find that all four eclipses—over both years—fell on the biblical holidays of Passover and the Feast of Tabernacles. I just about jumped out of my skin.

Immediately I ran to my computer and pulled up NASA's website to look up other times when there have been four consecutive blood moons, which are total lunar eclipses, where the moon appears blood red. NASA calls four total blood moons in a row a *tetrad*, and they list their occurrences. I noticed there weren't any in the 1600s, 1700s, or even the 1800s. The last time there was a tetrad was back in the 1900s, and to my amazement, they also fell on the feasts of Passover and Tabernacles.

When I noticed the years these phenomena occurred, my mind began reeling. The last two times there were four blood moons in a row, they happened, first, right after Israel became a nation in 1948, and then again when Israel retook Jerusalem in 1967. I started doing a hallelujah dance. It was as if I had just found treasure buried in the sand. My heart was racing a hundred miles an hour as all those key Scriptures about the signs in the heavens, God's feast days, and the timing on the biblical calendar flooded my mind.

This led me on an incredible journey of discovery as I began linking the feast days in the Bible with the signs in the heavens to when they fall on the biblical calendar. God said in Genesis 1:14 that He created the sun and moon and stars for *signals* on His feast days. Now I had a key to unlocking the code.

1
MY STORY

My parents, Harry and Jean Biltz, were devout Catholics. By the time they were twenty-nine and thirty, they already had nine kids. I was the second to last. We were raised in a very strict Catholic home in a small German Catholic town of about eight hundred people, known as Colwich, Kansas. We had the Stations of the Cross on the walls in our house and holy water at the entrances of the bedrooms. Of my five older sisters, three went through the convent, and of the four boys, three of us attended seminary. My oldest sister, Gayle, actually became a nun, though she left the order after a few years.

Our house was small, so my five older sisters shared one bedroom and we four boys shared the other. We only had one full bath for all eleven of us. It was a nightmare trying to get all of us ready for church.

My father was a successful salesman who by age twenty-nine owned his house outright and drove a brand-new VW van. One night in 1957, when my younger brother was a newborn and I was only a year and a half old, my dad was on his way home, when he had a terrible accident. Driving around fifty miles an hour, he crested a hill. And there it was, an abandoned truck, right in his lane on the highway. There was nothing he could do.

The accident nearly killed my father and even made national news. Dad was hospitalized and in a full-body cast for a couple of years.

At one point, tired of being away from his family, he called his friend (who owned a mortuary) to rescue him. His friend came to the hospital with his hearse and pretended to be picking up a dead body. While my dad played dead, his buddy wheeled him out on a gurney. The hospital staff thought my dad had died—until he called them later to see if they could pick him back up.

We found out later that the driver of the truck had been drinking and had run out of gas. Instead of pulling over onto the shoulder, he'd abandoned his truck right in the roadway. Worse, he didn't have auto insurance, so we had to use all of our savings on my dad's medical expenses.

When he was finally released from the hospital, he convalesced at home for a long time. He couldn't work for years, and my mother, with nine kids, including a newborn, to take care of, couldn't earn any money either. Eventually our money ran out, and we had to live on welfare. We used to joke that we were so poor you could look up the word *poor* in the dictionary and it would say, "SEE THE BILTZ FAMILY." My sister Kevin, in third grade, even had to wear boy's shoes that were donated to us. My mom told her they were women's army shoes, and they could make her run faster. When the kids at school made fun of Kevin, she would tell them she wore those special army shoes because they made girls run fast.

At Christmastime, the whole town would pitch in and bring us food and Christmas presents. Because the accident had gone around the world, in both the national news and the *Stars and Stripes* newspaper, we'd literally have two truckloads of toys and items delivered to our house. It was so crowded we couldn't walk in our living room.

My dad kept a positive attitude despite the fact that he was crippled. The wreck had completely destroyed his femur in his right leg, as well as his right hip. Prosthetics weren't nearly as advanced in 1957 as they are today. Doctors had to replace his femur with a metal rod, and they told him his leg would either be straight down or straight out. With no hip, the rod would remain in a permanent position, so he would have to decide if he wanted to stand or sit for the rest of his life. My dad said he wanted to stand, so he could look the world in the eye and never be able to sit again.

On top of all that, his right leg was two inches shorter than his left, so he had to wear a built-up shoe. Despite it all, he had a great sense of humor.

As he got better, my dad was constantly told that no one would hire a cripple, so he went to work for himself. When artificial hips came out, he had one put in so he could swing his leg. He also asked the doctors if they could lengthen his bad leg by two inches so he wouldn't need the special shoe. They said no but offered to shorten his good leg by two inches, so he went for that. They cut two inches of bone out of his left femur and then put brackets, nuts, and bolts in to hold it together till it healed. Before it was fully mended, he fell and broke it, so the doctors had to reset it. But eventually, with his right leg repaired, a new hip, and his legs the same length, he was good to go.

Through all of this, my mother, even with a houseful of kids and a husband unable to move for almost four years, somehow kept joy in the house. It was her servant's attitude and my father's positive outlook in spite of life's difficulties that made me who I am today. The years of taking care of our dad gave all of us a servant mentality. We did it, for the most part, with joy.

As his kids grew older, my dad hoped that one of us would become a priest or a nun. For a devout Catholic family, that is always the hope. A life-changing event in the eighth grade began to propel me in that direction.

Like most thirteen-year-olds who are going through hormonal changes, I experienced feelings of hopelessness. Because of situations at school, I decided to run away from home. We lived by a wooded area with a creek, near a highway and a set of railroad tracks that the hobos would hang around, waiting to hop on a train as it went by during the day. I grabbed my pillow, sleeping bag, and a backpack and headed off into the woods, ready to jump on the next train in the morning and see the world. I left a note on my bed, saying that nobody loved me, and that I was running away.

At the time, because my mom was off on a religious retreat, the only people at home were my dad; my sister Kevin, who was in high school; and my brother Tim, who was a year younger than me. They read the note and just knew I would be camping out in the woods by the creek. My dad, being crippled, couldn't go out and look for me, so he sent my brother and sister.

Tim and Kevin came to the creek and started calling

for me. In tears, I cried out to God, asking whether or not I should tell them where I was. Suddenly I heard a loud voice that sounded like my dad's, coming from a police bullhorn from the highway close by. He said to tell Tim and Kevin where I was. I immediately thought, *Dad must have had the police pick him up and drive him around to look for me.* Then I heard my brother's and sister's voices again, calling out for me, so I cried out to God a second time, asking whether or not I should answer them. Once more, my dad's booming voice called out and told me to tell my siblings where I was. At that point I cried out to them, and they came running over to me.

"Am I in trouble with the law for being a runaway?" I asked them. "Is Dad mad at me?"

"Dad's at home," they told me.

Only they had been looking for me.

"But I heard Dad's voice calling to me," I said.

They said they never heard a thing.

Just then, a very muscular man, around thirty and with a very kind face, came literally out of nowhere. Now, mind you, in my small town of eight hundred, some people had eighteen kids and there were only about a hundred families in all. Everybody knew everybody. Yet we had never seen this man. He asked if he could help, and my sister told him I had run away but had decided to go home. The man said that was good, because home is where I belonged. Then he left. We never saw him again. All three of us really believed this was an angelic visitation. It was important that I returned home to where I was loved.

Feeling now that God had a call on my life, I left home at thirteen, after graduating from grade school, to live in a dormitory at Savior of the World Seminary in Kansas City, Kansas. But after four years of being around only boys, and knowing that priests aren't allowed to marry, I said, "Forget this! I want to get married." So the following summer I left the seminary and went to a Catholic college in Wichita.

It was 1975, the year that my life took another major turn. For extra credit, I was helping my psychology teacher on campus with a court-mandated course with juvenile delinquents who had to attend the class. Our college campus had Ping-Pong tables, and I often played in tournaments. One day, a childhood friend of mine named Dan S., came by and asked if we could play Ping-Pong. But what he *really* wanted was to share with me how I could have a personal relationship with God. Just a few weeks earlier, I had called a monastery in Gethsemane, Kentucky, to tell them that I felt such an urge to be close to God that I wanted to become a Trappist monk. I told them my story: how I went through four years of seminary, thought I wanted to get married, but now decided otherwise. They told me to wait just one more year.

Dan's entire family had come to the Lord, and he invited me to the Assembly of God church he was going to that was having a revival and a guest speaker the next evening. I went, and that night I gave my heart to the Lord and never looked back.

It was a total shock to my family—especially to my parents, who were hoping for a priest. Not only did I not become a priest, but I also quit the Catholic Church. Instead I joined a youth organization known as the Agape Force, a parachurch organization made up of young adults who were involved in producing albums, doing street evangelism, helping juvenile delinquents, and the like.

One of my instructors over that time was David Wilkerson, who was my next-door neighbor for a short while. (I even had a chance to play Ping-Pong with him.) I also had the privilege of learning about the Gospel from Leonard Ravenhill, Winkie Pratney, and some other amazing teachers. Then, after a year and a half of traveling the United States with the Agape Force, I moved back to Wichita, Kansas. My friend Dan had joined a nondenominational charismatic church, the kind that were springing up everywhere in the 1970s. He recommended I join it with him. I agreed and even attended the church's small Bible college, where, eventually, I taught as well.

Years earlier, our family realized we had some Jewish roots on our father's side, but we could never really put our finger on anything till my younger brother, Tim, jumped full bore into looking into our genealogy. My father had always said that if he wasn't a Catholic, he would be Jewish. We even held a Passover Seder occasionally, growing up, and I still have my Haggadah from when we celebrated it. With Tim having discovered our Jewish roots, suddenly I felt as if studying the Old Testament in Bible college was like studying my own heritage.

One of the subjects my professors taught was the feasts of the Lord. I thought it was great. Later, as I reflected back on those times, it was amazing to me that they were teaching this subject back in 1975.

Since I was new to my friend's congregation—and because I was young and single—Dan's family wanted to introduce me to all the young ladies. It was there I met my future wife, Vicki Crowell.

For several months, Vicki really caught my eye. She was always smiling and seemed to be very outgoing. After a short while of trying to get my courage up to ask her out, I thought it would be easier instead to crash a lunch date she was having with someone else at a Pizza Hut. That day, I joined them at the table and put on the charm. (She remembers me telling "corny" jokes. I always thought they were good . . .) Soon we were a couple, and after dating for only a few months, we got engaged.

And then something terrible happened.

I've always believed my life was truly in God's hands, but that the devil is actively prowling the earth, seeking to thwart the Lord's workers. There were several instances in my life where I believe the devil almost succeeded. One of the more dramatic ones happened in 1977. On the Fourth of July, only a few weeks before I was to marry my beautiful bride, I stayed up late watching the fireworks show at Wichita State University. I had a paper route at the time (yes, my father-in-law was really excited his daughter was going to marry a paperboy), but because of the celebration, I didn't get enough sleep. At four in the morning, while driving down the highway in my step van, I fell asleep at the wheel. The vibrating of the rumble strips on the shoulder woke me just as a speed limit sign seemed to be coming right at me. Quickly I jerked the car to the left, and was then heading right into the ditch in the median. So I jerked the car hard to the right and rolled the van three and a half times, side over side, the length of a football field, and then landed in the middle of the ditch in the center median.

When I came to, I crawled out the driver's side window, hobbled to a nearby farmhouse, woke up the owner, and called my parents to pick me up. We finished delivering the papers, and then I went to the local doctor. He checked me out, and miraculously, all that was wrong with me were some scratches on my back and a sprained ankle. He wrapped my ankle and sent me home.

Some friends encouraged me to go to Wesley Hospital in the big city of Wichita, because they would do a more thorough check. There, technicians took an X-ray of my ankle and agreed it was only sprained, but they still wanted to put a cast on it. When they took off my ACE bandage, I mentioned that my ankle looked pretty puffy. They said it was because my bandage had been too tight.

So there I was, three weeks before my wedding, with a cast on my foot. At least they said it could come off by the wedding. Maybe things wouldn't be so bad after all, I thought.

That's when I developed a fever that spiked up to 105 degrees. I didn't know why I was so sick. My leg was killing me, and I couldn't work. I went back to Wesley Hospital and begged them to take off my cast. I said it was killing me, and that I had a terrible fever. They told me I just wasn't used to a cast and that malaria was causing the fever. They prescribed me some quinine and sent me home.

The day before my wedding, I was losing it. I went back to my family doctor and convinced him to cut open the cast enough to see if all was well. He finally acquiesced. When he began to open up my cast, we could see my ankle was all black and blue and abscessed. The doctor quickly cut off the cast, grabbed a knife, and slashed my ankle open to get all the infection out. He said that if he hadn't, I would have died the next day, on my wedding day, due to the infection in my bloodstream.

On our honeymoon, my wife had to push me in a wheelchair around Worlds of Fun in Kansas City. (I owe her one, she says.) But the devil did not prevail.

Another time I almost died was when I was robbed at gunpoint while managing a Payless shoe store in Wichita. It was the middle of the day, and I was alone in the store when the masked robber threatened me with a gun. After filling his bags with money from the cash register and safe, he took me in the back room and told me to lie down. I thought I was going to get a bullet in my head, but strangely, I was at peace. Proverbs 3:24–26 came to my mind: "When thou liest down, thou shalt not be afraid: yea, thou shalt lie down, and thy sleep shall be sweet. Be not afraid of sudden fear, neither of the desolation of the wicked, when it cometh. For the LORD shall be thy confidence, and shall keep thy foot from being taken."

The robber fled and my life was spared.

Then there were a couple of other times I almost died, from broadsiding a car that ran a red light to having a gun at my head again. I'll spare you the details, but the point is, through it all, the devil never prevailed against me. Not once.

Since my accident and the other life-threatening situations in which I have been involved, I have known beyond a shadow of a doubt that if it wasn't my time to go, it wasn't going to happen. These events have confirmed that belief. So I have become fearless. I will never test God, but I also know with absolute confidence that my life is in His hands.

My wife and I went on to have two sons, Christopher and Andrew. We only had two children because Vicki and I both came from large families, and we didn't want to be outnumbered. Over the next ten years, I continued to work in the shoe business: five years at Payless and then five years at Heads, a local shoe store in downtown Wichita.

Then, in 1987, one of our former pastors in Wichita who had moved to the Tacoma, Washington, area asked Vicki and me to join him. He wanted me to be his associate pastor. So we packed our bags and moved from Wichita to Washington. After a few years, that pastor ended up moving to Oregon and then back to Wichita. I took a position at another independent congregation in the Buckley area, where I administrated and taught in the Bible college. I was also an elder there.

By the time our boys were in high school, I was burned-out. For the last eighteen years, from 1975 to 1993, I'd not only worked full-time, but had volunteered many hours at the two churches.

When our pastor decided to retire, I helped vote in the next pastor, and then I decided it was time for a break. While I was not wrestling with my faith, I was just totally tapped out. Since I had a hard time not being involved, I thought it was best if I didn't go to church anywhere for an entire year. I wanted to focus on our boys. Vicki continued leading worship, and our boys tagged along, but I took a much-needed break.

It was in 1994, after my yearlong sabbatical, that Vicki bought me the book by Rabbi Moshe Braun, and it truly revolutionized my life. It was as though the lights suddenly came on, or like seeing a 3-D movie with the glasses on. I saw the Bible from a totally new perspective, and I just had to learn more. Instead of just wading through the Word, now I was scuba diving through the depths of the Scriptures. Here I had been to Bible college, taught in Bible college, and studied the feast days, but had come to find out I was still seeing "through a glass, darkly" (1 Cor. 13:12).

It turns out that the class I took on the feasts of the Lord back in 1977 was taught from a replacement theology perspective—that is, the idea that the church has replaced Israel, so all the promises to Israel now apply to the church. Desperately wanting to know more about the biblical feasts, I prayed that the Lord would send me somewhere that could point me in the right direction.

I happened upon a very small congregation in Puyallup, Washington, that introduced me to the authors, materials, and organizations I was looking for. I was an avid reader and studied like crazy. After attending that congregation for a few years and seeing many people come and go, I felt a desire to launch a congregation where I could teach what I was learning in a way that would be more palatable for Christians. By 2001, two other couples whom Vicki and I had known for years, Norm and Sue Belliveau and Bud and Cindy Flowers, convinced me it was time to start our own congregation. Norm had business experience, Sue had nonprofit expertise, and Bud and Cindy had a house where we could meet. Vicki led worship, and she was the one who came up with the name El Shaddai Ministries. I could stay focused on just teaching!

We started small, with just our three families, but we quickly grew to about twenty-five people and had to move into a small building, known as the Grange, nearby. After only a few months, we grew some more and had to move again. We found a small church that would rent to us. It worked out great, as we kept Shabbat and met on Saturdays, and they met on Sundays.

In just a few months, we grew to about seventy-five people and realized we needed to find a big enough place to really grow into. At that time, I was working part-time at a local Family Christian Bookstore. One of my coworkers told me we should talk to her church, as they might be willing to rent to us. So I did, and soon we had a home in South Hill Christian Church in Puyallup for the next couple of years.

At first, we had plenty of room in the sanctuary, but within two years we had grown from seventy-five to more than three hundred people.

Then another major turn of events!

2
SIGNS & SIGNALS

I t seems everywhere you turn, someone is looking for signs of intelligent extraterrestrial life that might be trying to communicate with us. Scientists spend hours and hours of time, as well as millions of dollars on research, to see if there is life anywhere else in the universe. We set up giant satellite dishes, trying to pick up any communication signals that might be sent our way. We are always looking for signs or signals, hoping that someone else just might be out there.

I do think it is amusing, though, that for the most part, the research scientists looking for E.T. totally ignore the greatest time in history when an Extraterrestrial spoke to three million people all at once who were all witnesses to the event. This heavenly Being who arrived on our planet at Mount Sinai even made sure they had a book written with all His insights on how to help humankind. Yet these scientists pay no attention to this recorded, major historic event.

God knows that we are creatures who always look for signs. That is why He uses many ways to get our attention. The problem is we don't always understand or know how to read the signs that He sends us. It's like the proverbial blind men trying to describe an elephant. One describes it as a wall, because he fell against its broad side. Another says it's like a spear, because he ran into the pointed tusk. A third man believes it's like a snake, because he felt the squirming trunk. Another describes it like a tree, because its legs are so round and thick. Yet another describes it as being like a fan because its ears are so thin and fluid. The last blind man describes the elephant as a rope, because he grabbed hold of the tail. Sometimes it's hard to grasp the whole because our perspectives are so skewed. So let's research some of the many different ways in the Bible that God uses to get our attention.

Isaiah 46:10 tells us that God declares *"the end from the beginning,* and from ancient times the things that are not yet done."* So if we want to know the end of a matter, we really need to start at the beginning and look at what God says. To understand prophecy, you don't want to start in Revelation, but in Genesis. There are more than three hundred references in the book of Revelation to the *Tanakh,* or Old Testament. If you throw out the Old Testament, you've just thrown away your reference manual to Revelation. From the declaration in Isaiah, we see that we need to look in Genesis to properly understand the future.

Proverbs 25:2 tells us, "It is the glory of God to conceal a thing: but the honour of kings is to search out a matter." God chose to hide His messages in the ancient Hebrew alphabet. You will find that the written Hebrew language is like the decoder ring to understanding what God is hiding.

Acts 3:19–21 says that the Messiah will remain in heaven until the restoration of all things spoken by the prophets. One item that has been restored after almost two thousand years is, coincidentally, the Hebrew language. The resurgence of Hebrew in a major way occurred at the beginning of the 1900s. What followed were two major world wars. Understanding this will help you better understand prophecy and how the return of the Hebrew language was a major sign for the times.

> Therefore wait ye upon me, saith the LORD, until the day that I rise up to the prey: for my determination is to gather the nations, that I may assemble the kingdoms, to pour upon them mine indignation, even all my fierce anger: for all the earth shall be devoured with the fire of my jealousy. For then will I turn to the people *a pure language*, that they may all call upon the name of the LORD, to serve him with one consent. (Zeph. 3:8–9)

It's as if a tower of Babel reversal is coming, and everyone will receive a free Hebrew download. I want to get an early start.

The Creator of the universe likes to play hide-and-seek, and God only reveals Himself to those who go on the hunt for Him. Anyone can say they love God while they pursue their own self-centered interests. But God will only reveal Himself to those who pursue *Him*. And even then it can't be a halfhearted pursuit.

When I was a child, we could not afford toys, so we would go to the library and check out books. I became an avid reader at a very early age. What I loved most were the Nancy Drew books, the Hardy Boys, and Tom Sawyer and Huckleberry Finn. I also read all the Dick Tracy material

I could get my hands on, because I wanted adventure and secret codes. In grade school I even made up my own secret language to communicate with my friends by simply adding "ong" to the consonants in a word.

Another thing I loved as a child was looking for the hidden pictures found in *Highlights* magazine. Today many pictures are created that either have hidden images within them or 3-D images popping out of them. Incredible art encoded with Hebrew fonts, words, and images can be found at the unique website www.hebrew-cypher-art.com. And anyone with an interest can find encoded biblical meanings by combining the numerical equivalents of each Hebrew letter in a word or phrase. Our God is the Supreme Encoder!

One piece of wisdom I tell people is, don't argue with a blind person over a work of art and don't argue with a deaf person over a piece of music. Others will see this or they won't. A blind person can't criticize the sighted person just because he doesn't see the picture. When I started looking at the Bible through the 3-D glasses of the Hebrew language, I could finally see the picture. I don't criticize those who don't see the whole picture, but I do invite you to join me in exploring the Bible from a whole, new, fresh perspective.

When I began studying Christianity's Jewish roots, I experienced the same thing as hundreds of other people whose eyes were opened. I felt as if I had been robbed all these years of understanding. "Why wasn't I ever taught this?" people would ask me when their eyes were finally opened. I have to tell them they can't be mad at their teachers, because people don't know what they don't know. How can you expect them to teach what they were never taught?

In the beginning God created the Hebrew alphabet, or *aleph-bet*. We see this from the Hebrew in the first verse of Genesis. A literal translation of the first four Hebrew words would be: "In the beginning God created את." This Hebrew word is not translated in your English Bibles. Hebrew is read right to left. In English this would be "*aleph, tav*." Better known as A to Z, the beginning and the end, the alpha and omega. We know God created the universe through speech. He spoke it into existence, and when He did, He used Hebrew. We know that words are made up of letters, but the amazing thing about the Hebrew language is, every letter is also a word, a number, and a picture. The Bible uses words where even the letters are symbols and signs.

One of my very favorite authors and teachers on the Hebrew aleph-bet, is Dr. Frank Seekins, who has written numerous books on the ancient picture language that God uses. One of them is simply called *Hebrew Word Pictures* (you can find out more about the pictorial and symbolic meaning of the Hebrew aleph-bet on his website, www.livingwordpictures.com). The first Hebrew letter is *aleph*, written א. It begins many of the Hebrew names for God that we translate into English, such as Elohim and Adonai. Being the first letter and representing that which is strong, in the ancient picture language it was drawn like the head of an ox: 𐤀. The ancient Hebrew letter ת (*tav*) looked like a cross ✝ or an ✗ in the Paleo-Hebrew alphabet. The letter tav means "mark" or "sign" as well as "covenant." It also represents a signature. This is why people often put an *x* for their signatures. Combined, these two Hebrew letters represent not only the entire Hebrew aleph-bet but they also represent God's signature. Pictorially it tells us that את is a *strong sign* ✝ ⌓.

Another powerful picture in the Hebrew aleph-bet is seen in the letter ו (*vav*). The letter vav looks like a nail used to connect things. That is exactly what it is. The word vav in the Bible is translated as "hook." In Hebrew it is used as a conjunction, like our word *and*, and is used to connect two words or thoughts. Interestingly enough, when you put the Hebrew letter vav between the two letters aleph and tav, you get the Hebrew word for sign: אות (*owth*). This is the same Hebrew word used in Genesis 1:14 when God declares He created the sun and moon for signs. This word אות is also the very same Hebrew word for the word *letter*. In other words, the Hebrew letters are to be signs! So, let's look at a few.

Like Dr. Seekins, I will start with some easy, basic, two-letter Hebrew words that everyone will understand. One of the Hebrew names for God is אל (*El*). As I pointed out earlier, the letter א (aleph) means "that which is first and strong." The letter ל (*lamed*) in the ancient picture language pictured a shepherd's staff and represented authority. So pictorially, when God's name was written, it represented the first and strong authority and looked like this: ⌓ℓ.

One of my other favorites is the Hebrew word for father. We are familiar with *Abba*, or *Daddy*, from Romans 8:15; the first two letters of that word—אב (*av*)—are the word for *father*. The letter ב (*beth*) in Hebrew means "house," and in the ancient picture language, Moses drew a three-room house for the letter. So the word for *father* was drawn as a picture of an ox and a house: ⊞⌓. This would show that

Father is the "strength of the house."

One of the most incredible signs in the Hebrew alephbet is found in the word for fire. We know God is a consuming fire. The Hebrew word for fire is אש (*esh*). The ancient letter ש (*shin*) looks like our *w* but represented as fangs and means "tooth." The concept of the letter is to consume or destroy. From the picture language, we see that fire is a "strong devourer": 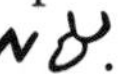. Since man and woman were created in God's image, they are also consuming fires. This reveals itself in the Hebrew words for man and woman. The Hebrew word for man is the word for fire, with the letter י (*yod*) in the middle: איש. The letter י means "hand" in Hebrew. In the ancient Hebrew, it looked like this: . Its position in the middle of the word for fire shows us that man (איש) works in or has his hand in the midst of the fire. The word for woman is also made up of the word for fire, as she too was created in God's image. For the Hebrew word for woman, you take the word for fire (אש) and add the Hebrew letter ה (*hey*). You now have the word אשה (*ishah*). The letter ה means "to reveal" or "that which comes out of." In the ancient Hebrew it looked like this: . So symbolically *woman* represents that which the fire reveals, or the one who comes out of the fire.

Now take note of God's name from Psalms 68:4: "Sing unto God, sing praises to his name: extol him that rideth upon the heavens by his name JAH and rejoice before him." The two letters making up God's name are the letters יה.

Let's look again at the two words for man and woman. What do we find? The common denominator of man and woman is fire אש. When a man and a woman get married and become husband and wife, we see the extra letters are what each brings into the marriage. The man brings the letter ' (yod), and the woman brings the letter ה (hey), and together it forms God's name: יה. This tells us that if *God* is not in our marriages, all we have is fire, and we consume each other. Only when a man and a woman come together is God capable of being in their midst, and only when God is in their midst can the couple thrive without consuming one another.

God's name, יה (*Jah* or *Yah*) in the picture language would have looked like this: ♈⊐ and meant the "hand revealed" or "behold the hand." I can't help but think of Yeshua's (Jesus') statement to doubting Thomas in John 20:27: "Then saith he to Thomas, Reach hither thy finger, and *behold my hands.*"

Most people are familiar with the Hebrew word *shalom*, which means "peace." However, only in the picture language do we find the deeper significance of that word. We know in the last days there will be a false peace, but how will we know the difference between a false peace and a true peace? To find the biblical meaning for peace, we must look at the symbolic meanings of the Hebrew letters. Here is the word *shalom* in Hebrew: שלום. Most of the letters you have already seen. Our new letter is the last letter of the word, ᴍᴍ (*mem*), which represents water. In the ancient picture language, it looked like a crashing wave of water, symbolizing chaos, like a tsunami.

Let's review. Remember that the Hebrew alphabet is read from right to left. So the first letter in shalom is ש (*shin*), which means "to consume or destroy." What does that have to do with peace? The next letter is ל (*lamed*), which represents authority. So the first two letters of the word for peace in Hebrew mean "destroying authority." The next letter is 1(vav), which means "to connect." This leaves us with the letter ᴧᴧ (mem), symbolizing chaos. So when we put all this together, we find that true peace, or shalom, comes only when you destroy the authority that is connected to the chaos! Biblical peace comes not from pacifism but from destroying those things that are bringing chaos to the world. When Satan's authority is destroyed, true peace will finally reign on earth.

Another great example of the rich symbolism in the Hebrew language is found in the word *Zion,* which is another name for Jerusalem. When King David wrote the word *Zion* in the ancient Hebrew, he used the letters whose corresponding picture signs have significant meaning, which is why I like to use the Hebrew name for Jesus, *Yeshua.* "Jesus" carries no meaning in itself other than as a reference to a historical person, but the name Yeshua literally means "God's salvation." So when Jesus's mother introduced him to people, she was saying, "Please meet my son, God's Salvation."

Yeshua said in the Gospels that He wanted to make His disciples fishers of men. The first letter of the Hebrew word for Zion is ׳ *(tsade).* This letter in the ancient picture language, ↗, looked like a fishhook, which is what it means. The last letter, ׀ *(nun)* looked like a fish darting through water, ↖, and represents life. So in ancient Hebrew the first letter of Zion was a fishhook, and the last letter was the picture of a fish darting through water. So what is the bait that will catch the fish? It's the middle two letters of the word for Zion! Those letters are *yood* (ᴗ◡ノ) and vav (1), or the picture of a hand and a nail! So the nailed hand of Yeshua is the bait on the hook to catch the fish אגד! He said, "If I be lifted up, . . . [I] will draw all men unto me" (John 12:32). It was in Zion that He was high and lifted up. All of this is too wonderful for me.

Many believers want nothing to do with the Torah. They treat it like the pop bottle in *The Gods Must Be Crazy*. In that movie a bottle was thrown from an airplane flying over the African plains. A native tribesman saw it land and thought it came from the gods in heaven. He took it back to his normally peaceful village, where everyone passed it around. The bottle was used for every purpose but that for which it was created. The villagers soon became envious of those who had the bottle. They fought over it and abused others with it. Eventually, they determined it would be best if they gave it back to the gods, so they selected a tribesman to take it to a faraway cliff thought to be the edge of the earth, where he threw it over the side. Sounds much like what has happened to the Torah.[1]

But the Torah is wonderful and good. Let me show you what God's encoded picture language tells us about it.

The first letter is ת (*tav*), which looked like our small letter *t* or a cross. The next letter is ו (vav), which resembles a nail. The next letter is ר (*resh*), which means "head," and it used to look like a person's head. It symbolizes the highest person or prince. The last letter is ה (*hey*), which means "to behold" or "reveal." Putting this all together we see the *Torah* is revealing the highest one nailed to the cross, or the sign of

---

1 The Hebrew word *Torah* is translated into English as *law*, when a better translation would be *instruction*.

the covenant! **ｷｶ1+** That is going left to right. But even going right to left, as Hebrew is written, we see the covenantal sign attached to the highest person revealed.

But there's more! The prophet Isaiah wrote that God declares the end from the beginning. There is no closer beginning to the beginning than the very first word in the Bible. The first three English words, *in the beginning,* are only one word in Hebrew: *B'reisheet* (בראשית.)

In Genesis, everything is in seed form and needs to be unpacked. The word *b'reisheet* could be separated this way: ראשית / ב. The Hebrew letter ב (*beth*) is the word for "in," and ראשית (*reisheet*) is translated as "beginning." So *b'reisheet* in Hebrew is translated into English as "in the beginning." While the letter ב means "in," "by," or "for," the word בית (*bayit*) means "house." Remember that in Hebrew every letter is also a word, so if you have a four-letter word, there are four words within it.

Why did God begin His greatest manuscript with these letters above all others? He began His story with the letter whose word meaning is "house" because it is the story of how He wants to build a house. One builds a house if he is expecting a family, so actually, it is more than a house; it is a home. At the opening of the Bible, you have the letter ב symbolizing the entrance to a house. Often a homeowner hides the key to the house somewhere by the entrance. God, as the Master Homeowner, has also hidden a key at the entrance of His house.

Most homeowners also have house keys on their key rings, but the house key is often one among many. And just as you need to have the *right* keys to get into all the doors of a house, you also need the right keys to unlock the many mysteries of the Bible. What you will receive by reading this book are absolutely critical keys to unlocking the secrets of the Bible that have been hidden from the masses for a very long time. While these have been known for a while in some circles, they have generally not been known by the body of the Messiah. What I will be sharing with you I received from others and am only standing on the shoulders of giants. For instance for the concept of the word for Yeshua and firstfruits mentioned here, I am grateful to Dr. Fass and his book, *Creation's Heartbeat* (see the bibliography).

Let's back up and look more closely at the word *reisheet* (ראשית). Before we do, though, I'd like to thank Frank Seekins for his work in Hebrew Word Pictures for explaining so well the picture language of ancient Hebrew. I had said *reisheet* was translated as "beginning." In Leviticus it is also translated as "firstfruits": "Speak unto the children of Israel, and say unto them, When ye be come into the land which I give unto you, and shall reap the harvest thereof, then ye shall bring *a sheaf* of the *firstfruits* [ראשית] of your harvest unto the priest" (Lev. 23:10).

In the New Testament, we see that one of the names for Messiah Yeshua is *reisheet*: "But each in his own order: *Messiah the first fruits*, [ראשית] then those who are Messiah's, at his coming" (1 Cor. 15:23 HNV). As I mentioned earlier, the letter ב (beth) could have also been translated with the English words *by* or *for*. So Genesis 1:1 could have been translated as "For the Messiah, . . ." or "By the Messiah, God created the heavens and the earth." And what do we find in the New Testament?

For *by him* [the Messiah] were all things created, that are in heaven, and that are in earth, visible and invisible, whether they be thrones, or dominions, or principalities, or powers: all things *were created by him, and for him.* (Col. 1:16)

In the book of Revelation, we read:

And all that dwell upon the earth shall worship him, whose names are not written in the book of life of *the Lamb slain from the foundation of the world.* (13:8)

The word *b'reisheet* (בראשית) is the very foundation of the world since, not only is it the first word; it even means "the beginning." It's the cornerstone of creation. So if Yeshua was "slain from the foundation of the world," we should be able to see within this Hebrew word that Yeshua was going to die! So let's unpack it.

The first two letters you find in the word *b'reisheet* form the word *bar* (בר). Bar is a very common word among the Jewish people. In Aramaic it means *son*, as in Daniel 3:25. But it can also mean grain, as in Genesis 41:49: "Yosef [Joseph] laid up *grain* as the sand of the sea, very much, until he stopped counting, for it was without number" (HNV).

We see a connection between this same word translated as both "son" and "grain" in the Gospel of John: "Yeshua answered them, 'The time has come for the *Son* of Man to be glorified. Most certainly I tell you, unless a *grain* of wheat falls into the *eretz* [earth] and dies, it remains by itself alone. But if it dies, it bears much fruit (John 12:23–24 HNV).

If you add the next letter in *b'reisheet* (בראשית), the

letter א (aleph), you get another Hebrew word, *bara* (ברא), which is the word for "created" in Genesis 1:1. And according to Colossians 1:16, the *Son* was the one who *created* all things: "For *by him were all things created.*"

You probably have heard the term Rosh Hashanah. *Rosh* (ראש) is the Hebrew word for "head." This word is used in Deuteronomy 28:13: "And the LORD shall make thee the *head,* [ראש] and not the tail." When you add the letter י (yod) to the end of the word *rosh* (ראשי), it becomes "*my* head." We also find this added letter in the middle of the word *b'reisheet* (ב / ראשי / ת). Then we discover this in Ephesians 1:22 concerning Yeshua:

> He put all things in subjection under his feet, and gave him to *be head* over all things for the assembly. (HNV)

Let's look at what we have so far from the word *b'reisheet* (בראשית):

בראשית In the beginning
בר the *Son*
ברא *created* all things
ראשי on *My Head*

Now if you take the word בראשית and cut it in half, you get ברא / שית. The last three letters (שית) in English are translated as "thorns," as we see in Isaiah 10:17: "And the light of Israel shall be for a fire, and his Holy One for a flame: and it shall burn and devour his *thorns* [שית] and his briers in one day."

So now we have: "The *Son* / who *created* / all things / on *my head* / a crown of *thorns*."

Remember when we separated the word *b'resheet* like this: ראשית / ב? We saw that we have the word *reisheet* (ראשית), which means "firstfruit," and that the word *bar* (בר) means "grain." So we also learn from this word that Yeshua was the "grain of the firstfruits offering." I could go on for hours, and have. You can watch twenty-two hours of me teaching on the Hebrew aleph-bet. (See the resource section on page 176 for information on how to watch the videos.) I spent an hour on each letter, going over the word meaning, the picture meaning, and the numerical value. If you view this teaching, you will also learn how the Messiah is seen in each letter. You'll definitely have a great handle on the aleph-bet when you're done.

Now that I have shown you how God uses the Hebrew aleph-bet as signs, let's move on to the signs in the earth and heavens. The Bible plainly declares there will be signs in the heavens, especially concerning the end of time, as we know it. This especially makes sense now that we understand that it's why God created the heavenly bodies in the first place! So let's look at some of the references:

> For the stars of heaven and the constellations thereof shall not give their light: *the sun shall be darkened in his going forth, and the moon shall not cause her light to shine.* (Isa. 13:10)

> And I will shew *wonders in the heavens and in the earth,* blood, and fire, and pillars of smoke. *The sun shall be turned into darkness, and the moon into blood, before* the great and the terrible day of the LORD come. And it shall

come to pass, that whosoever shall call on the name of the LORD shall be delivered: for in mount Zion and in Jerusalem shall be deliverance, as the LORD hath said, and in the remnant whom the LORD shall call. (Joel 2:30–32)

The *sun and the moon shall be darkened*, and *the stars* shall withdraw their shining. (Joel 3:15)

And great earthquakes shall be in divers places, and famines, and pestilences; and fearful sights and *great signs shall there be from heaven*. (Luke 21:11)

And there shall be *signs in the sun, and in the moon*, and in the stars; and upon the earth distress of nations, with perplexity; the sea and the waves roaring. (Luke 21:25)

And I beheld when he had opened the sixth seal, and, lo, there was a great earthquake; and *the sun became black as sackcloth of hair, and the moon became as blood*. (Rev. 6:12)

Why would we expect anything different? The Bible declares from the very beginning that God created the sun, the moon, and the stars *to send us signals!* How can anyone deny the significance of these signals?

God is and has always been in complete control of the heavenly bodies. We see this in Joshua 10:13–14:

And *the sun stood still, and the moon stayed*, until the people had avenged themselves upon their enemies. Is not this written in the book of Jasher? So the *sun stood still in the midst of heaven, and hasted not to go down about a whole day*. And there was no day like that before it or after it, that the LORD hearkened unto the voice of a man: for the LORD fought for Israel.

We also see God controlling the sun when Hezekiah wanted a sign from God that He would lengthen the king's life:

> And Isaiah said, *This sign shalt thou have of the LORD*, that the LORD will do the thing that he hath spoken: shall the shadow go forward ten degrees, or go back ten degrees? And Hezekiah answered, It is a light thing for the shadow to go down ten degrees: nay, but *let the shadow return backward ten degrees*. And Isaiah the prophet cried unto the LORD: and he brought the shadow ten degrees backward, by which it had gone down in the dial of Ahaz. (2 Kings 20:9–11)

We see it again when Yeshua was on the cross. Matthew wrote: "Now from the sixth hour *there was darkness over all the land* unto the ninth hour" (Matt. 27:45). This was definitely a supernatural darkness, because Yeshua died in the middle of the month on the biblical calendar, and you can only have a total solar eclipse at the beginning of a biblical month. So it couldn't have been a solar eclipse. Furthermore, total solar eclipses never last for three hours. So this was totally a divinely created darkness.

The Babylonian Talmud, written almost two thousand years ago, records in Jewish thinking that whenever the sun is in total eclipse, it is a bad omen for the nations. When the moon is in total eclipse, it is a bad omen for Israel. All throughout history, civilizations such as the Egyptians and the Mayans have looked to the heavens for patterns and celestial signs, trying to understand if they portend coming events on earth. Eclipses have always had a profound effect on people. I believe God placed the wonder in our DNA so we would try to understand what He is saying. If you read James Ussher's *The Annals of the World*, you will see the profound impact eclipses have had on mankind's thinking.

Let's move on and look at prophecy buffs' favorite portion of Matthew:

> And as he sat upon the mount of Olives, the disciples came unto him privately, saying, Tell us, when shall these things be? and what shall *be the sign of thy coming*, and of the end of the world? (Matt. 24:3)

Yeshua then spends the rest of the chapter listing a multitude of signs, from wars to famines, pestilences, and even earthquakes. But there is one aspect of this entire chapter that is totally missed if one does not understand the culture and context of that day. If you had been one of the disciples that were around as Yeshua explained the signs to come, one detail would have leapt out. Chanukah was going to happen again! Yeshua kept Chanukah and even used it as the platform to explain He was the Messiah:

> And it was at Jerusalem *the feast of the dedication,* and *it was winter.* And Jesus walked in the temple in Solomon's porch. Then came the Jews round about him, and said unto him, How long dost thou make us to doubt? If thou be the Christ, tell us plainly. (John 10:22–24)

The word for "dedication" in Hebrew is *Chanukah,* which happens in winter!

Let's look at all the references to the signs of Chanukah in Matthew 24:

- "And then shall many be offended, and shall betray one another, and shall hate one another" (Matt. 24:10). As you read the stories of the Maccabees, and even in *The Works of Josephus*, you can see the records of the betrayal of Jews against Jews.

- "And because iniquity shall abound, the love of many shall wax cold" (Matt. 24:12). This is exactly what happened, as iniquity here implies lawlessness or being without the Torah.

- "When ye therefore shall see the abomination of desolation, spoken of by Daniel the prophet, stand in the holy place, (whoso readeth, let him understand:) Then let them which be in Judaea flee into the mountains" (Matt. 24:15–16). This had already been fulfilled during Chanukah, around 168 BC. Josephus even stated that what Antiochus did in desecrating the Temple and setting up in it an idol in it was the fulfillment of Daniel's prophecy. I believe that when the Bible says here, "whoso readeth, let him understand," it is warning that the events around Chanukah will happen again. Historically people fled to the mountains to escape.

- "But pray ye that your flight be not in the winter, neither on the sabbath day" (Matt. 24:20). Chanukah is in the winter! It was on the Sabbath that the Jews did not fight back and were slaughtered. It was at this point in history that the Jewish people declared it was lawful to defend your life on the Sabbath. This whole conversation was like a giant flashing billboard declaring Chanukah will happen again in the future when the Antichrist defiles the Temple and sets up an idol in it.

I like to ask people, "What was the difference between Haman of the book of Esther and Antiochus Epiphanes of Chanukah?" Haman was all about *annihilation,* wanting to kill every Jew, no matter what. Antiochus Epiphanes, on the other hand, was all about *assimilation.* One of the great signs of the last days will be assimilation, for example, the Chrislam, which is a merging of Christianity and Islam, that you see being promoted today.

The Antichrist's goal will also be assimilation. You will only be annihilated if you don't assimilate.

- "For there shall arise false Christs, and false prophets, and shall shew great signs and wonders; insomuch that, if it were possible, they shall deceive the very elect" (Matt. 24:24). Wow! Did you catch that? Not only will God and His prophets be showing great signs and wonders; so will the false messiahs and false prophets. How will you know which ones are true prophets when both are performing great signs and wonders? You better understand the litmus test or you will never know until it's too late. Many people think they can determine if a prophet is a true one or not by whether what he prophesies takes place. That is not totally accurate. God may be testing you to see if you know the litmus test. You can find it in Deuteronomy 13.

- "Immediately after the tribulation of those days shall the sun be darkened, and the moon shall not give her light, and the stars shall fall from heaven, and the powers of the heavens shall be shaken." (Matt. 24:29). Now, this is definitely a supernatural sign-in-the-heavens event!

- "But as the days of Noe were, so shall also the coming of the Son of man be" (Matt. 24:37). When I read this I see the biblical calendar all over the place. God is telling you to get on His calendar. Let me explain.

Noah was long before Moses, so in his time the first month was the month of Tishri rather than Nisan. So when you adjust your thinking to the biblical calendar in Noah's day, what do you find?

In the six hundredth year of Noah's life, *in the second month, the seventeenth day of the month*, the same day were all the fountains of the great deep broken up, and the windows of heaven were opened. And the rain was upon the earth *forty days and forty nights.* (Gen. 7:11–12)

The second month is Cheshvan, similar to our late October–early November time frame. So it was the seventeenth day of this month that the rain started. When you count forward forty days, you come to Kislev 27. The rain stops and a beautiful rainbow appears. And on the biblical calendar, Kislev 27 is right in the middle of Chanukah! Then what do we find?

And the waters returned from off the earth continually: and after the end of the hundred and fifty days the waters were abated. And the ark rested in the seventh month, *on the seventeenth day of the month*, upon the mountains of Ararat. (Gen. 8:3–4)

The seventh month at that time was Nisan. We know Passover is celebrated on the fourteenth of Nisan. Yeshua rose on the seventeenth of Nisan, the same day the ark rested!

And it came to pass in the six hundredth and first year, *in the first month, the first day of the month*, the waters were dried up from off the earth: and Noah removed the covering of the ark, and looked, and, behold, the face of the ground was dry. (Gen. 8:13)

The first day of the first month is Rosh Hashanah—the very day Adam was created and proclaimed God as King! When I see that during the end times it will be like it was in the days of Noah, I'm going to be looking at the biblical calendar and remembering Chanukah.

Now that we've seen all of these Matthew 24 passages, let's look at Luke 17:28–29:

Likewise also as it was *in the days of Lot*; they did eat, they drank, they bought, they sold, they planted, they builded; But *the same day* that Lot went out of Sodom it rained fire and brimstone from heaven, and destroyed them all.

When did this event happen on the calendar? There's a big clue in the text and from Jewish records. First look at God's conversation with Abraham in Genesis 18:

> And the LORD said unto Abraham, Wherefore did Sarah laugh, saying, Shall I of a surety bear a child, which am old? Is any thing too hard for the LORD? At *the time appointed* I will return unto thee, according to the time of life, and Sarah shall have a son. (vv. 13–14)

The Hebrew word for "appointed time" here is *moed*, which is the very word God uses for His feast days. It is taught that a year later Isaac was born, and it was on the Feast of Passover. We know that after Passover comes the seven-day Feast of Unleavened Bread. So what was Lot serving the angelic host who came down to save him?

> And he pressed upon them greatly; and they turned in unto him, and entered into his house; and he made them a *feast, and did bake unleavened bread*, and they did eat. (Gen. 19:3)

So if the time of the Messiah's coming is to be as it was in the days of Lot, could similar events happen during Passover some other year?

When it comes to understanding biblical prophecy, we are on a treasure hunt, mining the Scriptures and leaving no stone unturned as we look for answers regarding things to come. First Peter 1:12 even declares that the angels strongly desire to look into such mysteries. Just imagine: the angels in heaven are having a Bible study, trying to figure out all of this right along with us!

Looking back at Genesis 1:14, if we closely examine the text, we see that there are actually four reasons the lights in the heavens were created:

> And God said, Let there be lights in the firmament of the heaven to divide the day from the night; and let them be for *signs*, and for *seasons*, and for *days*, and *years*.

In Hebrew, we learned the word for signs is *owth* (אות) and this word carries the meaning of sending signals. Think of a lighthouse on a dark and stormy night, trying to warn mariners of impending disaster. God created the sun and the moon as His own personal transmitters! This would be unbelievable if it wasn't true! The question is, are we tuning in?

If you are a baseball fan, then when you are watching a game, you might see a coach patting his hat or his leg to signal to the base runner whether or not he is to steal a base. What happens if the runner doesn't know the signal? There will be consequences! It's the same with God's children. God desires to warn us of impending calamities. He always warns before He brings judgment.

This verse in Genesis had never really hit me before as it does now. If you are a believer in the Bible, and God says He created the sun and the moon to send signals, then you just have to believe it.

The indescribable Creator of this magnificent universe loves His creation passionately and wants to communicate with us. Our Abba Father wants the entire world to know He exists, so He created the world as the nursery, and the heavens are what He painted on the ceiling of our room so that when we, as His children, gaze heavenward, we would see His glory. This is why Psalms 19:1 says that "the heavens *declare* the glory of God."

The Hebrew word for our English word *declare* actually means "to celebrate and to be inscribed in the heavens." The verse goes on to say that "the firmament *shows* His handywork." This means from the Hebrew "to boldly announce, to rehearse, and to be a messenger." This is so mind-blowing to me! Here the heavens are literally God's canvas, and He is the Supreme Artist and Creator. We can look to the heavens and read His story. The heavenly host, including the constellations, are celebrating, telling, and rehearsing the entire plan of the Creator for human history!

But before you get too excited about the constellations, note that there is a big difference between biblical astronomy and astrology. In astrology, humans falsely assume it's all about them, and then they end up worshipping the created rather than the Creator. We see this in the book of Acts:

> And when the people saw what Paul had done, they lifted up their voices, saying in the speech of Lycaonia, The gods are come down to us in the likeness of men. And they called Barnabas, *Jupiter*; and Paul, *Mercurius*, because he was the chief speaker. Then the priest of Jupiter, which was before their city, brought oxen and garlands unto the gates, and would have done sacrifice with the people.

Which when the apostles, Barnabas and Paul, heard of, they rent their clothes, and ran in among the people, crying out, And saying, Sirs, why do ye these things? We also are men of like passions with you, and preach unto you that ye should *turn from these vanities* unto the living God, which made heaven, and earth, and the sea, and all things that are therein: Who in times past suffered all nations to walk in their own ways. (14:11–16)

This verse shows us the Galatians worshipped the planets as we see in their calling Barnabas, Jupiter and Paul, Mercurius and in thinking they were the gods of these planets. It is so important for us to realize that it was the Galatians who worshipped the planets, and Paul told them to turn from these vanities. You will see in an upcoming chapter where I will go into more detail on this, but for now I want you to realize that the devil always defiles and perverts everything God does, and then many end up throwing out the baby with the bathwater, so to speak. In the late 1800s, E. W. Bullinger wrote a book called *Witness of the Stars* showing how the heavens are actually proclaiming the Good News and lays out for us the Gospel from beginning to end. There is nothing wrong with admiring the majesty of God in the heavens as long as we understand it is His Story, not ours!

What is so incredible about Psalm 19 is that it goes on to say:

Day unto day uttereth speech, and night unto night showeth knowledge. There is no speech nor language, where their voice is not heard. Their line is gone out through all the earth, and their words to the end of the world. In them hath he set a tabernacle for the sun, which is as a bridegroom coming out of his chamber, and rejoiceth as a strong man to run a race. His going forth is from the end of the heaven. (vv. 2–6)

To "reveal" in this verse implies it is "living it out." There is knowledge to be obtained in understanding God's perspective of the heavenly host. At night, the constellations are living out God's plan, not ours! So, God wrote His story in the heavens to "declare," or show, what is to come! This is what the heavens are revealing! When it says their "line" has gone out through all the earth, in the Hebrew it implies that this is a "chorus line," as if all the heavens are singing forth God's praises and speaking forth His glory! We just need to be tuned in to the right channel.

The Hebrew word for "canopy" is *chuppah*, which is what the bridegroom and bride get married under in a Jewish wedding. God is coming for His bride, and He has set the day of His wedding. The saying goes, "Always a bridesmaid and never the bride." Do you want to be a part of the bride? Then I suggest you learn the Groom's signals, come to God's feasts by getting on His calendar, and then enjoy His dress rehearsals!

Everything in the heavens is declaring the coming of the Messiah for His bride. Are we listening to what they are saying? In Psalms 89:37, God says the moon is His faithful witness in the heavens. It testifies of His covenantal faithfulness to the seed of King David and that it will be one of his seed who will rule on the throne in Jerusalem, the undivided capital of Israel!

The Scripture also says there is no speech or language

where the language of the heavens is not heard. How absolutely amazing our God is! There are more than 6 billion people on this planet, speaking hundreds, if not thousands, of different languages, so He chooses signs that everyone can see and understand, no matter what their language is. But He chooses signs we must look for, that are beyond the control and manipulation of any human. There's never a lack of prophetic charlatans in this world; that's for sure!

Allow me to show you some remarkable insights into the Scriptures concerning biblical astronomy. There are billions upon billions of stars, and the amazing thing is the Bible dramatically mentions the names of some of these stars and constellations in several places.

Job 38:31–32 says, "Canst thou bind the sweet influences of Pleiades, or loose the bands of Orion?" Here we have the mention of the Seven Sisters or the seven stars known as the Pleiades as well as the constellation Orion. As a matter of fact, God has given names to all the stars!

The Psalmist says that He calls *all* the stars "by their names" (Ps. 147:4). The Bible also talks about the Lord binding and loosing the constellations and bringing forth the seasons. He even controls the waters:

> Seek him that maketh *the seven stars and Orion*, and turneth the shadow of death into the morning, and maketh the day dark with night: that calleth for the waters of the sea, and poureth them out upon the face of the earth: The LORD is his name. (Amos 5:8)

When Job mentions Arcturus, Orion, and Pleiades in Job 9:9, he is referring to the star, Arcturus, located in the constellation Boötes as well as the constellation Orion and the seven stars making up the Pleiades.

In the book of Revelation, John wrote that the Lord "had in his right hand seven stars" (Rev. 1:16). I believe Pleiades is what is being referred to here as well. From Bullinger's book the *Witness of the Stars*, we find that the Syriac name for the Pleiades is *Succoth*, which means "booths." *Pleiades* means "*the congregation* of the judge, or ruler." This is incredible—especially since Pleiades is found within Taurus, the Bull! And here we have the Seven Sisters within the constellation Taurus, showing they are the congregation of the Ruler!

If you look up the Hebrew word for Arcturus, you will see it means "to assemble." As a matter of fact, the same Hebrew word translated as Arcturus is even translated as the word "assemble" in Joel 3:11 of the Christian Bible: "*Assemble* yourselves, and *come*."

What is amazing to me is that Arcturus is the brightest star in the constellation Boötes. This is correctly pronounced with three syllables, as Bō•ō•teez. I say this because the Hebrew word *Bo* means "to come"—the concept we see in the same verse. The constellation Boötes represents the coming of the Messiah. It is pictured as a man walking rapidly, with a spear in his right hand and a sickle in his left hand. You see this being referred to in Psalms: "Then shall all the trees of the wood rejoice before the LORD: for *he cometh, for he cometh to judge* the earth: he shall judge the world with righteousness, and the people with his truth" (Ps. 96:12–13).

Now let's read from verses 11–16 in Joel 3 and you will see the coming of the Lord acted out in the heavens, which truly do declare the glory of God!

43

Assemble yourselves, and come [*Bo*] all ye heathen, and gather yourselves together round about: thither cause thy mighty ones to *come down*, O LORD. Let the heathen be wakened, and come up to the valley of Jehoshaphat: for there will I sit *to judge* all the heathen round about. *Put ye in the sickle*, for the harvest is ripe: *come*, get you down; for the press is full, the fats overflow; for their wickedness is great. Multitudes, multitudes in the valley of decision: for *the day of the LORD* is near in the valley of decision. *The sun and the moon shall be darkened*, and the stars shall withdraw their shining. The LORD also shall roar out of Zion, and utter his voice from Jerusalem; and the heavens and the earth shall shake: but the LORD will be the hope of his people, and the strength of the children of Israel.

In this passage, we have both the Hebrew word for Arcturus, *assemble*, and the word *to come*, or *Bo*. So there we see the constellation Boötes—the man with a sickle in hand, coming to judge the earth!

In Matthew 24, the disciples ask Yeshua, "What shall be the sign of thy coming?" Here's part of Yeshua's response:

Immediately after the tribulation of those days shall *the sun be darkened, and the moon shall not give her light*, and *the stars shall fall from heaven*, and the powers of the heavens shall be shaken: And then shall appear the sign of the Son of man in heaven: and then shall all the tribes of the earth mourn, and they shall see the Son of man coming in the clouds of heaven with power and great glory. And he shall send his angels with a great sound of a trumpet, and they shall gather together his elect from the four winds, from one end of heaven to the other. Now learn a *parable of the fig tree*; When his branch is yet tender, and putteth forth leaves, ye know that summer is nigh: So likewise ye, when ye shall see all these things, know that it is near, even at the doors. Verily I say unto you, *This generation shall not pass*, till all these things be fulfilled. (Matt. 24:29–34)

There is so much packed in these verses I can only speak to some of it. First off, some Christians, because they have cut themselves out of the tree Israel rather than being grafted in, think God made a new tree and planted it in some other country. They don't realize Matthew 24 is all about the story of Chanukah happening again. We know from the Scriptures that Israel is the fig tree (see Hosea 9:10; Joel 1:7; and Jeremiah 24:5). We also know that Israel's becoming a nation in May 1948, when summer was literally just around the corner, was the fulfillment of prophecy. Many students of Scripture wonder how long a biblical generation is. There are many possibilities, but one thing is for sure: when Israel captured Jerusalem in 1967, that was another giant leap forward in fulfilled prophecy.

Let's see the connection of this event with Scripture:

When the LORD shall build up Zion, he shall appear in his glory. (Ps. 102:16)

It was one thing for Israel to become a nation, and quite another to recapture Jerusalem and see it built up. Zion is another name for Jerusalem. The Scriptures say that when this event happens, the Lord shall appear in His glory! So for whom was this written?

The next verse says: "This shall be written *for the generation to come*" (Ps 102:18). The Hebrew word for this phrase implies that it is for the *terminal generation*, or the last generation! We are that generation!

We have seen Zion built up. We have seen Jerusalem reunited into Jewish hands. Heaven forbid Israel ever divides it.

3
SEASONS: SPRING FEASTS

Why did God create the sun and the moon? In chapter 2, we learned that the heavenly bodies are signs pointing to something significant when they fall on the feast days. In this chapter, we will discover *what* they point toward.

Genesis 1:14 tells us, "And God said, Let there be lights in the firmament of the heaven to divide the day from the night; and let them be for signs, and *for seasons* [מועד], and for days, and years" (Gen. 1:14). In our Western mind-set we figure God is talking about winter, spring, summer, and fall. This is far from accurate. Though the translators interpreted the Hebrew word *moed* (מועד) in Genesis to mean "seasons," this same Hebrew word in Leviticus 23 has been translated as something different:

> And the LORD spake unto Moses, saying, Speak unto the children of Israel, and say unto them, Concerning the feasts [מועד] of the LORD, which ye shall proclaim to be holy *convocations*, even these are *my feasts*. (vv. 2–3)

Now, when I think of a feast, I imagine a big, fat turkey, casseroles, and pumpkin pies. The "feasts" God wanted Moses to discuss with the Israelites were also holidays, like Passover, Shavuot/Pentecost, and Yom Kippur. In the Bible, there are spring feasts and fall feasts. In this chapter, I focus on the spring feasts, the dress rehearsals of which have already happened. I'll explain in a minute. In the next chapters, I'll cover the fall feasts, which are the ones we need to prepare for to be ready.

So, here we have the English translators rendering the same Hebrew word, moed, using two completely different English words: *seasons* and *feasts.* In our culture, these two words don't seem to go together. So what does the word *moed* really mean? Is it great food or is it one of the seasons? Actually, neither! In the Hebrew language, the word is more accurately translated as "divine appointment." This is incredible!

Many people believe in divine appointments, but did you ever imagine that there are scheduled ones? The Creator of the universe declares that He wants to interact with us at set times. It's as if God has an appointment book that He uses to keep track of when He wants to interact with us humans. Being in a "Hebrew mind-set" and having a basic understanding of the Hebrew language when reading your Bible will help you understand these appointments. The feasts of the Lord are the divine appointments, when God predetermined that He would intersect with human history. So God has told us that He created the sun and the moon not only to send signals but also to determine His feast days, or appointed times. This is why the sun and moon operate like clockwork. If we want to know where we are in history according to God's prophetic time clock, then we need to go by God's clock, not ours.

If you look closely, you will see that the last two Hebrew letters of this word מועד are *ayin* (ע) and *dalet* (ד), which mean "an eternal witness forever." The feasts of the Lord are His eternal witnesses, just like the sun and the moon, which He uses as His signals on those very feast days!

Some people say that the feasts of the Lord aren't important anymore, that they were done away with in the New Testament. But God is the God of yesterday, today, and forever. If you throw out the feast days, you have just thrown out one of your decoder rings! No wonder that in Daniel's vision he saw the Antichrist speaking against God and trying to "change times" (Dan. 7:25). This is referring to God's appointed times.

When God is about to be up to something big, He will send us signals via the sun and the moon on His feast days. This is huge! Get hold of this and it will revolutionize your walk with God because you will be walking in agreement with Him on His schedule.

What would your boss do if he told you he wanted to meet with you on Thursday at 4:00 p.m., and you told him that you just might if you could work it into your schedule? Let's go a step further. Let's say you tell him that Monday at 2:00 p.m. works better for you, and maybe he should change his schedule. We all know it doesn't work that way, especially if you want to remain employed. Now hear this: the sovereign Lord has already told us when He wants to meet with us. Who are we to tell Him that He needs to change

His schedule and meet with us at our own convenience?

Here is the definition of moed from *Strong's Concordance*:

Feast: moed מועד

#4150 an appointment, i.e., a fixed *time or season*; . . . also *a signal (as* appointed *beforehand); appointed* (sign, time).

The feasts by themselves, like the celestial bodies, are to be signals, agreed upon beforehand. If you have entered the covenant of God's family, then you are supposed to know the family's signals. But the feasts were also to be holy convocations. In Hebrew, the word for convocation is *miqra* (מקרא), and *Strong's* defines *miqra* as not only an assembly but also a rehearsal (think, *dress* rehearsal!):

#4744 from 7121; something called out, i.e. a public meeting, also *a rehearsal.*

When it comes to being part of the wedding of the Messiah, do you want to be the bride or the bridesmaid? All of us who are passionate in our relationships with God want to be at the wedding feast. Let me ask you, then: don't you think it would be a good idea to also be at the dress rehearsal? Then get ready to go on one of the rides of your theological life. The feasts of the Lord were and are to be dress rehearsals of coming events.

Let's look at the feasts.

SPRING FEASTS

FESTIVAL	CELEBRATING	JEWISH MONTH	GREGORIAN MONTH
PASSOVER	THE LORD'S DEATH	NISAN	MARCH–APRIL
UNLEAVENED BREAD	THE LORD'S BURIAL	NISAN	MARCH–APRIL
FIRSTFRUITS	THE RESURRECTION	NISAN	MARCH–APRIL
PENTECOST	GIVING OF THE TORAH	SIVAN	MAY–JUNE

Passover

> In the fourteenth day of the first month at even is the
> LORD's Passover. (Lev. 23:5)

Every year for fifteen hundred years, Israel slew the Passover
lamb on the fourteenth day of Nisan. Specifically, the lamb
was slain at the time of the evening sacrifice. Why do you
think Messiah died on Passover at the time of the evening
sacrifice? Why do you think there were miraculous signs
in the heavens at that time? The odds of this happening,
as well as all the details I am going to show you, will blow
your mind.[1]

Do you remember that after Yeshua's Passover Seder
meal, He and His disciples sang a song? Mark records that
"when they had sung an hymn, they went out into the mount
of Olives" (Mark 14:26). What would you say if I told you
that I knew the words to the song they sang and that you
most likely have the hymnbook? It's really no surprise, since

---

1   I don't have space to go into all the details surrounding the crucifixion, but you
     can learn more on my feast DVDs (see resources on page 176).

the Jews sang the psalms at Passover. In particular, they would sing what is known as the Hallel, which is Psalms 113–118. So the last hymn they would have sung before Jesus was betrayed would have been Psalm 118:

> I will praise thee: for thou hast heard me, and art *become my salvation*. The *stone which the builders refused* is become the head stone of the corner. This is the LORD's doing; it is marvellous in our eyes. (vv. 21–23)

Here, just before He is betrayed and rejected, these are the words they are singing! The Messiah's rejection and His crucifixion were the Lord's doing, so you really can't blame the Jews. Also, remember the crucifixion is called the Lord's Passover. The Jews as a whole did not kill Yeshua; a few of them condemned him, but it was the gentiles who crucified Him as you see here:

> Behold, we go up to Jerusalem; and the Son of man shall be betrayed unto the chief priests and unto the scribes, and they shall condemn him to death, and shall deliver him *to the Gentiles to mock, and to scourge, and to crucify him*: and the third day he shall rise again. (Matt. 20:18–19)

The day after Yeshua was tried by Pilate and sent to be crucified, we find a very specific appointment:

> And they compel[led] one Simon a Cyrenian, who passed by, coming out of the country, the father of Alexander and Rufus, to bear his [Yeshua's] cross . . . And it was *the third hour*, and they *crucified him*. (Mark 15:21, 25)

On God's time clock, the third hour of the day is 9:00 a.m., the time of the morning sacrifice. So what is going on in the Temple this Passover morning? The Passover lamb that will be sacrificed that afternoon is being bound to the horns of the altar. At that same time, Yeshua is being nailed to the execution stake. And the Jews are singing the Hallel! Josephus, the Jewish historian who lived in that century, records that there were two-and-a-half million Jews there for Passover.[1] Can you imagine the beautiful singing of that choir? So what are the words to the song that Yeshua is hearing while He is being bound to the cross?

> God is the Lord, which hath shewed us light: bind the sacrifice with cords, even unto the horns of the altar. (Ps. 118:27)

The sixth hour of the day is 12:00 p.m., and the ninth hour is 3:00 p.m., which is the time of the evening sacrifice. And what happens?

> Now from *the sixth hour* there was darkness over all the land unto *the ninth hour.* And about the ninth hour Jesus cried with a loud voice, saying, Eli, Eli, lama sabachthani? that is to say, My God, my God, why hast thou forsaken me? (Matt. 27:45–46)

According to Acts 3:1 the ninth hour is the time for prayer. It is also the time of the evening sacrifice. And what are the multitudes singing?

---

1   *The Works of Josephus Complete and Unabridged | Antiquities of the Jews | Book* 6.9.3.425, p. 749.

The Lord [is] my strength and song, and is become my salvation. The voice of rejoicing and salvation [is] in the tabernacles of the righteous: the right hand of the Lord doeth valiantly. The right hand of the Lord is exalted: the right hand of the Lord doeth valiantly. (Ps. 118:14–16)

Yeshua died at the same time of the evening sacrifice. Do you see the dress rehearsals? The Creator of the universe predetermined when His Son would die, not only to the day but also to the very hour. He even decided what songs were to be sung at His funeral by giving King David the words through prophecy. These are God's appointed times. He keeps His appointments and is always on time.

There is a Jewish mourning ritual known as *keriah*, which is the tearing of one's clothes. The Bible records many instances of rending the clothes after news of a relative's death. When Jacob saw Joseph's coat of many colors drenched with what he thought to be his son's blood, he rent his garments. The most striking Jewish expression of grief is the rending of garments by the mourner prior to the burial of his loved one. The requirement of the mourner is to "expose the heart,"* the tear in the apparel representing his torn heart.[1] When Yeshua died on the cross, what happened?

And, behold, *the veil of the temple was rent in twain from the top to the bottom*; and the earth did quake, and the rocks rent. (Matt. 27:51)

---

1   Maurice Lamb, "Keriah—The Rending of Garments," Chabad.org, accessed November 26, 2013, http://www.chabad.org/library/article_cdo/aid/281558/jewish/Keriah-The-Rending-of-Garments.htm.

The Father is rending His garment from top to bottom, demonstrating His broken heart as He mourns the death of His Son.

Feast of Unleavened Bread

Leviticus 23:5–6 tells us that the fourteenth day of the first month is the Lord's Passover. Then we are told that the next day begins the Feast of Unleavened Bread. It was on this same fifteenth day of the first month that the Egyptians buried their firstborn after the Lord "had smitten them" just before the Israelites' exodus from Egypt (Num. 33:3–4).

Once the people reached the land God had promised them, they would each be required to give "a sheaf [or, omer] of the firstfruits" to the priests as a sacrifice: "When ye be come into the land which I give unto you, and shall reap the harvest thereof, then ye shall bring a *sheaf of the firstfruits* of your harvest unto the priest" (Lev. 23:10). In the Bible, a sheaf represents a person, and multiple sheaves indicate a number of people:

> For, behold, we were *binding sheaves* in the field, and, lo, my sheaf arose, and also stood upright; and, behold, your sheaves stood round about, and made obeisance to *my sheaf.* (Gen. 37:7)

> He that goeth forth and weepeth, bearing precious seed, shall doubtless come again with rejoicing, *bringing his sheaves* with him. (Ps. 126:6)

So this fifteenth day of the first month, the same day the Egyptians buried their firstborn, was the same day the

Messiah was in the grave, representing the firstborn of His creation. We also know the Messiah was "unleavened," or, without sin:

> For thou wilt not leave my soul in hell; neither wilt thou suffer thine *Holy One* to see corruption. (Ps. 16:10)

> For we have not an high priest which cannot be touched with the feeling of our infirmities; but was in all points tempted like as we are, yet without sin. (Heb. 4:25)

> For he hath made him to be sin for us, who knew no sin; that we might be made the righteousness of God in him. (2 Cor. 5:21)

Feast of Firstfruits

Amid the seven-day Feast of Unleavened Bread was another feast, known as the Feast of Firstfruits. It involved waving the firstfruits of the barley harvest in the Temple.

> And he shall wave the sheaf before the LORD, to be accepted for you: *on the morrow after the sabbath* the priest shall wave it. (Lev. 23:11)

The morning after the Sabbath, the two Marys came to the sepulcher to anoint Jesus's body, but an angel tells them: "Don't be afraid, for I know that you seek Yeshua, who has been crucified. He is not here, *for he has risen*, just like he said" (Matt. 28:5–6 HNV). Just as the Levitical high priest waved the "sheaf" of the firstfruits before the Lord, the Messiah was in the heavenly Temple, waving to the Father as the first Sheaf:

But now Messiah has been raised from the dead. He became *the first fruits* of those who are asleep. For since death came by man, the resurrection of the dead also came by man. For as in Adam all die, so also in Messiah all will be made alive. But each in his own order: Messiah the first fruits, then those who are Messiah's, at his coming. (1 Cor. 15:20–24 HNV)

God was loudly proclaiming, "Dress rehearsal!" Yeshua died on Passover, on the fourteenth of Nisan, not a month before or after, and even at the specified hour. He was buried on the fifteenth of Nisan, during the Feast of Unleavened Bread. He rose during the Feast of Firstfruits! How can anyone not see this as totally a God thing?

So what comes next on the biblical calendar?

Feast of Pentecost (Feast of Weeks)

After the firstfruits were waved before the Lord as an offering, the Israelites were to count seven weeks from the day the omer or sheaf was brought into the Temple:

> And ye shall count unto you from the morrow after the sabbath, from the day that ye brought the sheaf of the wave offering; seven sabbaths shall be complete: Even unto the morrow after the seventh sabbath shall ye number fifty days . . . Ye shall bring out of your habitations two wave loaves of two tenth deals: they shall be of fine flour; they shall be baked with leaven; they are the firstfruits unto the LORD. (Lev. 23:15–17)

Beginning on the day that the first omer of barley was harvested and brought to the Temple, a countdown to the next biblical festival began. The Israelites were commanded to count off forty-nine days and then celebrate the festival of Shavuot, or Feast of Weeks. Christians know it as the Feast of Pentecost. Everything that happened after the resurrection to the Feast of Pentecost occurred during the counting of the omer. For instance, the Ascension took place on the fortieth day of the counting of the omer: "And he led them [the disciples] out as far as to Bethany, and he lifted up his hands, and blessed them. And it came to pass, while he blessed them, he was parted from them, and carried up into heaven. And they worshipped him, and returned to Jerusalem with great joy: and *were continually in the temple*, praising and blessing God. Amen" (Luke 24:50–53). Notice that they were continually *in the Temple*, not in hiding.

When I was a child, I remember the church service being in Latin, and I was clueless at what was being said. As I grew older, I heard people say that the religious leaders liked to keep the laity in the dark about what the Bible really said, as a matter of control. The translation of the Bible into the common languages was and is very significant, as is the presentation of the Gospel in people's native tongues. But the problem still exists in that much of the laity wants to be spoon-fed the sweet "cookies and ice cream" feel-good messages and still have no clue what the Bible really says. Do you know many Christians today, and even a whole lot of pastors, don't actually know that the first Pentecost was not in the book of Acts? The Jews had been keeping the Feast of Pentecost already for fifteen hundred years! They were even commanded to:

> Three times in a year shall all thy males appear before the LORD thy God in the place which he shall choose; in the feast of unleavened bread, and in *the feast of weeks*, and in the feast of tabernacles: and they shall not appear before the LORD empty. (Deut. 16:16)

Fast-forward to the New Testament. We know from Acts 2:5–6 that on the day of Pentecost "there were dwelling at Jerusalem Jews, devout men, out of every nation under heaven . . . Every man heard them speak in his own language" (Acts 2:5–6).

Do you catch it? This was a Jewish event! The Jewish men from all nations were required to be at the Temple for the Feast of Pentecost. They all heard the disciples speaking in the language of their native countries. It's not as if three thousand *pagans* had just left the Temple prostitutes and were zapped and believed in God. The *Jews* were the first Pentecostals! I don't know of any Pentecostals who use Acts as their foundation that keep the feast or even know when it occurs on the biblical calendar. Yet to this day, the Jews still keep the feast! They stay up all night reading their Bibles! What do we see but another dress rehearsal, this time waving two leavened loaves?

> And the priest shall wave them with the bread of the firstfruits for a wave offering before the LORD, with the two lambs: they shall be holy to the LORD for the priest. And ye shall proclaim on the selfsame day, that it may be a holy *convocation* unto you. (Lev. 23:20–21)

Remember, a *convocation* is not only an assembly at an appointed time but also a dress rehearsal. So let's see how this is fulfilled.

Acts 2:1 says, "When the day of Pentecost was fully come, they were all with one accord in one place." This was not the Upper Room of Acts 1, but the open court in the Temple. (The Temple was known as God's house. Jesus said in Matthew 21:13, "It is written, *My house* shall be called *the house* of prayer.") After the Holy Ghost falls, as Jesus had promised, Peter declares to the confounded multitude that the disciples "are not drunken, as ye suppose, seeing it is *but the third hour* of the day" (Acts 2:15). So it's a large gathering at the third hour—that's 9 a.m., the time of the morning sacrifice on the Feast of Shavuot! Look at the impeccable timing again. The Feast of Shavuot (or Feast of Weeks) was also known as the Feast of Harvest:

> Three times thou shalt keep a feast unto me in the year. Thou shalt keep the *feast of unleavened bread*: (thou shalt eat unleavened bread seven days, as I commanded thee, in the time appointed of the month Abib; for in it thou camest out from Egypt: and none shall appear before me empty:) And *the feast of harvest*, the firstfruits of thy labours, which thou hast sown in the field: and the *feast of ingathering*, which is in the end of the year, when thou hast gathered in thy labours out of the field. (Ex. 23:14–16)

A few verses later, we see another dress rehearsal (convocation): "Then they that gladly received his word were baptized: and the same day there were added unto them about *three thousand souls*. And they continued steadfastly in the apostles' doctrine and fellowship, and in breaking of bread, and *in prayers*" (Acts 2:41–42). It was at this dress rehearsal that many "heard the word [and] believed; and the number of the men was about five thousand" (Acts 4:4). What a harvest on the Feast of Harvest, with more to come!

Multitudes of Jews were coming to faith during this time. Acts 21:20 tells us that "[tens of] thousands of Jews" believed, and they were "all zealous of the law." These Jews still loved and kept the Torah. They not only were coming to faith in Yeshua, but they were keeping the Old Testament law too. The "number of the disciples multiplied in Jerusalem greatly; and a great company of *the priests were obedient to the faith*" (Acts 6:7). They continued as priests in the Temple for the next forty years, until it was destroyed.

Notice this verse doesn't say, "former priests." These were all sons of Aaron who remained both Jewish and obedient to the faith in the Messiah.

Here comes a test. This is only a test. Do you believe that God is the same yesterday, today, and forever? If you said yes, you halfway passed the test. Let me qualify this. Do you believe with all your heart, mind, soul, and strength that God is the same yesterday, today, and forever, with no shadow of turning? Are you sure? Absolutely? Then let me ask you something. Do you believe that if God fulfilled the spring feasts, not only to the very day but to the very hour of His first coming then, He will fulfill the fall feasts to the very day of His second coming?

Prophecy students, it is imperative you get on God's calendar, or how will you know when the fall feasts are fulfilled?

The spring feasts were fulfilled in order: Jesus died on Passover, was buried during Unleavened Bread, was resurrected during Firstfruits, and the Spirit was poured out on Shavuot/Pentecost, bringing in the great harvest. So the fall feasts have to be fulfilled to the very days and in order! We are not setting dates here, as we have no idea what year the fulfillment will happen. We are just going by God's pattern. Before the Spirit could be poured out, Messiah had to rise from the dead. He could not rise before He was buried. He wouldn't be buried until He died. It is the same with the fall feasts. And most believers don't know anything about the fall feasts or when they occur on the biblical calendar to help them be aware of when they are fulfilled. So without delay let's move on to the fall feasts.

The first fall feast is the Feast of Trumpets, also known as Rosh Hashanah. Do you remember reading anything about trumpets in the book of Revelation? That is the next feast to be fulfilled. You should know when it comes every year! Then comes the Feast of Yom Kippur, which is Israel's national day of atonement. After that comes the Feast of Tabernacles, where God will tabernacle among men for one thousand years.

The fall harvest is no longer about barley and wheat. It is the grape harvest, and look at what we find in the book of Revelation:

> And another angel came out from the altar, which had power over fire; and cried with a loud cry to him that had the sharp sickle, saying, Thrust in thy sharp sickle,

and gather the *clusters of the vine* of the earth; *for her grapes are fully ripe.* (Rev. 14:18)

Just as the spring feasts were the dress rehearsals for Messiah's first coming; the fall feasts are the dress rehearsals for His second coming! And just as the spring feasts were all fulfilled in the spring to the very day of the biblical calendar, so the fall feasts will be fulfilled in the fall to the very day on the biblical calendar. The biblical calendar is one of the tools you need to properly understand what is quickly coming on the world.

Now that you are on the edge of your prophetic seats, let's take a look at the fall feasts and see what are the likely events that will happen on those very days in some coming year.

Wouldn't you want to know in advance of a major catastrophe that would impact your life? Wouldn't you like to be told when a tornado was about to strike your house or when the stock market was about to tank? Sure, we have developed some warning systems for weather events, and there are prognosticators who try to predict economic disasters, but no one really knows for sure. God, however, always warns before He brings judgment. In His mercy, He is sending big-time warnings from His heavenly billboards. You can ignore them at your own peril, pooh-pooh them and try to ride out the storm, or you can come to the dress rehearsals and be prepared for what is coming! Time is running short to proclaim the good news of Yeshua the Messiah. We can be paralyzed with fear about the signs, or excited as the finish line is in sight. We are in the final laps of this race. Yeshua, speaking of His second coming, asked if He would find faith on earth (Luke 18:8). The dress rehearsals are to increase our faith. Are we excited or what?

4
SEASONS: FALL FEASTS

I n chapter 2, we learned that God uses the heavenly
bodies as signs to let us know something big is going
to happen. In the last chapter, we saw how the spring
feasts were used as signs pointing to the death, burial,
and resurrection of Yeshua, and the outpouring of the
Holy Spirit at Pentecost. In this chapter, we will find out
what the fall feasts point toward and how to be prepared.

When it comes to the final three, the fall feasts, let's
first get the overall view. The first is the Feast of Trumpets,
held on the first of Tishri. The theme of this feast is *repentance*. Next comes the Feast of Yom Kippur on the tenth of
Tishri. This feast speaks of *redemption*. Finally comes the
Feast of Tabernacles, on the fifteenth of Tishri, which lasts
for seven days. *Rejoicing* is the theme of this feast. So, first
comes repentance, followed by redemption, which leads to
rejoicing! The feasts are in perfect order, just as the spring
feasts were.

FALL FEASTS

FESTIVAL	CELEBRATING	JEWISH MONTH	GREGORIAN MONTH
FEAST OF TRUMPETS	COMING KING	1ST OF TISHRI	SEPT–OCT
FEAST OF YOM KIPPUR	NATIONAL DAY OF ATONEMENT	10TH OF TISHRI	SEPT–OCT
FEAST OF TABERNACLES	GOD DWELLING WITH US	15TH OF TISHRI	SEPT–OCT

Feast of Trumpets (Yom Teruah)

Rather than rely on what man says about the feasts, let's see how the Creator describes His fall feasts:

> And the LORD spake unto Moses, saying, Speak unto the children of Israel, saying, In the *seventh month*, in the *first day of the month*, shall ye have a *Sabbath*, a *memorial* of *blowing* of *trumpets*, an holy *convocation*. (Lev. 23:23–24)

Okay, a couple of things to note here. Even if the first day of the seventh month falls on a day of the week other than Saturday, it is still considered a Sabbath. It is possible on God's calendar to have as many as four Sabbaths in a two-week time period. Next we see it is to be a memorial. In the United States, we think of Memorial Day as a way to remember our fallen soldiers. In Hebrew, the word for memorial is *zakar* and, according to *Strong's*, it means "to mark (so as *to be recognized*)" or "to be mindful" and "make to be remembered." God is asking us to set this day apart. If we remember Him, He will remember us. If the Lord has no remembrance of a person (or nation), then He has rejected him: "But he shall say, I tell you, I know you not whence ye are; depart from me, all ye workers of iniquity" (Luke 13:27). As a young man in love will give his girlfriend a locket with his picture in it as a memento, so God has given us this feast so we will remember Him. The problem is, God's people have lost the memento. How do you think that makes God feel? Well, how would it make *us* feel? We don't care when a stranger doesn't remember our birthdays or anniversaries, but when our spouses forget, that is different. How much more valuable is the Lord than your spouse? When God asks His family to remember something, we ought to remember. We don't want to be like the people in Jeremiah's time who had forgotten the Lord's days. The verse doesn't say they had forgotten the Lord's *days* but they had forgotten *Him* for "days without number." If you want this verse to include the feasts without naming them, since the verse doesn't, how about this: We don't want to be like the people in Jeremiah's day who had forgotten the Lord as mentioned in Jeremiah 2:32.

On the Feast of Trumpets, the shofar, or trumpet, is blown one hundred times. Three sounds are made with the trumpet: *Tekiah* is one long, straight blast. *Shevarim* is three shorter blasts. *Teruah* is nine quick blasts in short succession. The one hundredth blast on the Feast of Trumpets is known as "the last trump."

Paul wrote to the Corinthians, revealing a mystery: "We shall not all sleep, but we shall all be changed, in a moment, in the twinkling of an eye, *at the last trump*: for the trumpet shall sound, *and the dead shall be raised incorruptible*, and we shall be changed" (1 Cor. 15:51–53). When Paul said at "the last trump," he was referring to the hundredth blast on the Feast of Trumpets!

As I mentioned, God wants to be remembered. Don't you want your friends to remember your birthday or anniversary or special occasions? My goal is to help you find the lost treasure of God's feasts and His calendar! When we remember God by blowing the shofar on the Feast of Trumpets, God hears it and He remembers us. In fact, the Bible says that even in times of trouble, when we sound the trumpet, He remembers us: "And if ye go to war in your land against the enemy that oppresseth you, then ye shall *blow an alarm with the trumpets*; and *ye shall be remembered* before the LORD your God, and ye shall be saved from your enemies" (Num. 10:9). Don't you want to be remembered by God when you are in trouble?

As a reminder of divine mercy, every year on the first of Tishri, the Jews read the story of the binding of Isaac. They also blow the ram's horn to remind God of His mercy. This feast is a day to both remind people to repent of their sins and to remind God of His mercy.

The Feast of Trumpets actually has several names. Just as we might refer to Thanksgiving as Turkey Day, here are other names for this biblical feast.

The Time of Jacob's Trouble (The Day of the Lord)

The Day of the Awakening Blast

Yom HaDin (Day of Judgment/The Opening of the Books/Opening of the Gates)

Yom HaKeseh (The Hidden Day)

Ha Kiddushin/Nesuin (Wedding of the Messiah)

HaMelech (Coronation of the Messiah)

You may be familiar with some of these names. You may also be familiar with the term Rosh Hashanah, which means "the head of the year." But the biblical name for Rosh Hashanah is *Yom Teruah*, translated as "Day of Blowing." We find this in the book of Numbers:

> And in the *seventh* month, on the *first day of the month*, ye shall have an *holy convocation*; ye shall do no servile work: it is a *day [yom] of blowing [teruah]* the *trumpets [shofars]* unto you. (Num. 29:1)

This word *teruah* means "a battle cry," "sounding an alarm," and even "shouting," as seen in Psalms 47: "God is gone up with a shout [teruah], the LORD with the sound of a trumpet [*shofar*]" (v. 5). This verse shows the divine connection of the blowing of the shofar with Yom Teruah. In the New Testament, we see the blowing of the shofar being associated with the resurrection of the dead: "For the *Lord himself* shall descend from heaven *with a shout*, with the voice of the archangel, and with *the trump of God*: and *the dead in Christ shall rise first*" (1 Thess. 4:16). This is telling us the resurrection of the dead will happen at the Feast of Trumpets! I will prove this more as we go. For now, let's look at some of the other names that will help us on this amazing treasure hunt.

The Time of Jacob's Trouble/The Day of the LORD

Let's look at some verses that imply that the day of the LORD is also known as "Jacob's Trouble."

> Ask ye now, and see whether a man doth travail with child? wherefore do I see every man with his hands on his loins, *as a woman in travail*, and all faces are turned into paleness? Alas! for *that day is great*, so that none is like it: it is even the *time of Jacob's trouble*; but he shall be saved out of it. (Jer. 30:6–7)

> Howl ye; *for the day of the LORD* is at hand; it shall come as a destruction from the Almighty. Therefore shall all hands be faint, and every man's heart shall melt: And they shall be afraid: *pangs and sorrows shall take hold of them*; they shall be in pain *as a woman that travaileth*: they shall be amazed one at another; their faces shall be as flames. (Isa. 13:6–8)

This concept is carried over into the New Testament in Matthew 24:7–8: "For nation shall rise against nation, and kingdom against kingdom: and there shall be famines, and pestilences, and earthquakes, in divers places. All these are the beginning of *sorrows*." The Greek word *odin*, interpreted as "sorrows," implies here birth pangs. We see this also in the book of Daniel.

> And at that time shall Michael stand up, the great prince which standeth for the children of thy people: and there shall be *a time of trouble*, such as never was since there was a nation even to that same time: and *at that time thy people shall be delivered*, every one that shall be found *written in the book*. (Dan. 12:1)

Thankfully, there will be deliverance for God's people, in some fashion—and they will need it, because Zephaniah tells us that the Day of the LORD will be a time of trouble:

> The great day [*yom*] of the LORD is near, it is near, and hasteth greatly, even the voice of the day of the LORD: the mighty man shall cry there bitterly. That day is a *day of wrath, a day of trouble and distress*, a *day of wasteness and desolation*, a *day of darkness and gloominess*, a *day of clouds and thick darkness*, A *day of the trumpet* [*shofar*] *and alarm* [*teruah*] against the fenced cities, and against the high towers. (Zeph. 1:14–16)

Do you see the connection here between the day of the LORD and the shofars blown on Yom Teruah? I believe the time of trouble, or the Tribulation, will start in some year on the Feast of Trumpets! This passage will help us make the divine connection in this event. We see this in Joel too:

> *Blow ye the trumpet* [*shofar*] in Zion, and *sound an alarm* [*teruah*] in my holy mountain: let all the inhabitants of the land tremble: for *the day of the LORD cometh*, for it is nigh at hand; a *day of* darkness *and of gloominess*, a day of clouds and of *thick darkness*, as the morning spread upon the mountains: a great people and a strong; there hath not been ever the like, neither shall be any more after it, even to the years of many generations. (2:1–2)

The Day of the Awakening Blast

The Feast of Trumpets is also known as the Day of the Awakening Blast. This comes from the Scriptures. We already saw the connection with the Lord's return and the trumpet blast in 1 Thessalonians. Now let's look at some connections in the Tanakh:

> And many of them that *sleep in the dust of the earth shall awake*, some to everlasting life, and some to shame and everlasting contempt. (Dan. 12:2)

> Thy dead men shall live, together with my dead body shall they arise. Awake and sing, ye that dwell in dust: for thy dew is as the dew of herbs, and the earth shall cast out the dead. Come, my people, *enter thou into thy chambers, and shut thy doors* about thee: *hide thyself* as it were for a little moment, until the indignation be overpast. For, behold, the LORD cometh out of his place to punish the inhabitants of the earth for their iniquity: the earth also shall disclose her blood, and *shall no more cover her slain*. (Isa. 26:19–21)

The word *teruah,* if you remember, implies sounding an alarm. It is like an alarm clock going off to wake the dead. Rise and shine! Here is the bride of the Messiah, in the Song of Songs, who is spiritually asleep and needs to wake up:

[Woman]
I was sleeping, but my heart was awake.
A sound! My love is knocking:

[Man]
"Open for me, my sister, my dearest,
my dove, my perfect one!
My head is soaked with dew,
my hair, with the night mists."

[Woman]
"I have taken off my tunic—
     why should I put it on again?
I have bathed my feet—
     why should I get them dirty?" . . .
I went and opened for my love,
     but my love had turned, gone away. (Song 5:2–3, 6
CEB)

I find it interesting that the same Hebrew word used in Daniel 12:2 for those who "sleep" in the dust of the earth is also used here in the Song of Songs. It's as if the bride—the body of Messiah—is dead asleep when the Messiah comes to the door and knocks! We see the bride is not awake or eagerly anticipating the return of the Groom. Look at her apathy even when He does knock. She basically tells Him to take a hike, as she doesn't even want to put forth the effort to get out of the bed and put on her coat and shoes. When she finally opens the door, He's gone! This could be the fate of those who are apathetic and asleep.

Solomon is actually a type of the Antichrist, or Anti-Messiah. This may come as a shock to most, but this is why, if it were possible, even the elect would be deceived. Solomon did the opposite of everything God required (see Deuteronomy 17:16–17). He multiplied wives, many of them foreign; hoarded silver and gold; amassed horses; and built pagan altars for his foreign wives rather than destroying them. He was also an arms merchant, buying chariots and even giving them to the enemy. First Kings 10:14 tells us that the weight of gold that came into his kingdom yearly was 666 talents. People have some romantic ideal about

Solomon being a good, wise king, when instead he was evil and turned his back on God even after God appeared to him twice concerning his behavior. That is why God ripped the kingdom from him. Solomon even tried to give away twenty cities around the Galilee. He was so arrogant that he thought *he* had the authority to give away the Promised Land!

Land for peace . . . Does that sound familiar?

But it was the same in Solomon's time as it is now: the deal was rejected then, and the Palestinians continue to reject it today. It's all a God thing!

When you properly understand God's calendar and the feasts, you will realize that the Feast of Unleavened Bread, which falls on Nisan 15, is always during a full moon, as is the Feast of Tabernacles, on Tishri 15. But the Feast of Trumpets, which falls on Tishri 1, is always during a new moon. Because of the Diaspora (the scattering of Jews in other nations), it was celebrated for two days but was known as one long day. Why was it two days long? It fell on the first, the new moon, and everyone needed to know when it would begin, especially those in other countries, and it took a while for their notification. They would light torches on the hilltops to pass the word on. It's easy to determine when a feast is when it falls in the middle of the month. You just start with the first day of the month and keep counting. But how do you know when the first is? Because it was based on the Temple declaration in Jerusalem and on the sighting of two witnesses, no one knew for sure the day or the hour the Feast of Trumpets would begin.

So far we have looked at two different aspects of the

Feast of Trumpets. It is the day when the Great Tribulation begins, and it is also the day of the resurrection of the dead. Here is something extremely important to realize. These two events and the next few events that follow this feast day don't necessarily all happen the same year. I believe they will all take place on this day, but could very well occur in different years. There are actually multiple fulfillments to the feasts that I will show as we go. So let's continue with some of the other aspects of this feast.

Yom HaDin (Day of Judgment)

The next group of names for the Feast of Trumpets is known as Yom HaDin, or the Day of Judgment, the Opening of the Books, or the Opening of the Gates. In Judaism, it is believed that every year on Yom HaDin, the books are opened and the heavenly court is in session. God looks over every person's account to see how we took care of what He invested in us. The trial lasts ten days, until the Day of Atonement. The idea is for us to realize that our lives are placed on the balance scales. The trial image captures the sense of one's life in someone else's hands. Unless we repent and put our trust in Messiah's work on the cross, we will be judged according to our deeds. We have ten days to repent and amend our ways during this time before the judgment is set and the books are closed on Yom Kippur. Everyone in the world passes before the heavenly Judge, just like a general looking over his troops. The sentence is then meted out during the following days and year. We see the court setting and the opening of the books in Daniel:

A fiery stream issued and came forth from before him: thousand thousands ministered unto him, and *ten thousand times ten thousand* stood before him: *the judgment was set, and the books were opened.* I beheld then *because of the voice of the great words which the horn spake*: I beheld even till the beast was slain, and his body destroyed, and given to the burning flame. (Dan. 7:10–11)

This concept appears in the New Testament as well:

For we must all appear before the *judgment seat of Christ*; that every one may receive the things done in his body, according to that he hath done, whether it be good or bad. (2 Cor. 5:10)

In the book of Revelation, the Judge is sitting upon His throne:

And I saw a great white throne, and him that sat on it, from whose face the earth and the heaven fled away; and there was found no place for them. And I saw the dead, small and great, stand before God; and *the books were opened*: and another book was opened, which is the book of life: and the dead were judged out of those things which were *written in the books*, according to their works. (Rev. 20:11–12)

To summarize this section, the Feast of the Trumpet represents a time of trouble, an awakening blast, and the Day of Judgment. Now we will see how it is a day of hiding; when the heat is turned up, God will hide those whom He loves.

Yom HaKeseh

The Feast of the Trumpet is also called *Yom HaKeseh* or the Hidden Day. When people think about the Lord's wrath being poured out, they want to be hidden in a safe place. How many of you want to be hidden in the time of trouble and the day of the Lord's anger? Even the psalmist took comfort from the fact that "in the time of trouble he shall hide me in his pavilion: in the secret of his tabernacle shall he hide me; he shall set me up upon a rock" (Ps. 27:5).

When I was living in Kansas, sirens would go off to warn residents when a tornado was spotted. When you heard the siren, you were smart to find a safe place to hide as quickly as possible. I was one of those crazy guys who wanted to see the tornado in action. One time I was in the front yard, looking at a funnel cloud forming off in the distance, while my mother was shouting for me to get into the basement because a weatherman said a tornado had been spotted in our area and that everyone should take cover. Just as my mother heeded the weatherman's warning, *we'd* better listen when God proclaims disaster is near. When He announces three times that it is near, we'd really better listen to the warning; it is no false alarm!

Look at what the prophet Zephaniah says concerning warning signs and the great day of the Lord:

> The great day of the Lord *is near, it is near, and hasteth greatly*, even the voice of the day of the Lord: the mighty man shall cry there bitterly. That day is a day of wrath, a day of trouble and distress, a day of wasteness and desolation, a day of darkness and gloominess, a day of clouds and thick darkness, a *day of the trumpet and* alarm

against the fenced cities, and against the high towers. And I will bring distress upon men, that they shall walk like blind men, because they have sinned against the LORD: and their blood shall be poured out as dust, and their flesh as the dung. Neither their silver nor their gold shall be able to deliver them in the day of the LORD's wrath; but the whole land shall be devoured by the fire of his jealousy: for he shall make even a speedy riddance of all them that dwell in the land. (Zeph. 1:14–18)

Tied together again are Yom Teruah and the shofar blowing, as well the destruction of the high towers. I can't help but think of the twin towers that fell in New York City. In the first chapter of Zephaniah, the Lord is telling the Israelites to hurry, hurry, hurry. In the next chapter, He tells them what to do just before the disaster comes:

Gather yourselves together, yea, gather together, O nation not desired; *before* the decree bring forth, *before* the day pass as the chaff, *before* the fierce anger of the LORD come upon you, *before* the day of the LORD's anger come upon you. *Seek ye the LORD*, all ye meek of the earth, which have wrought his judgment; *seek righteousness, seek meekness*: it may be ye shall be *hid in the day of the LORD's anger.* (Zeph. 2:1–3)

Wow! If we believe that we are the terminal generation, then we'd better hurry up and we'd better be seeking the Lord, His righteousness, and meekness if we want to be hidden. One of the signs that we are ever so close to this great day of the Lord is found in the very next verse in Zephaniah: "For Gaza shall be forsaken, and Ashkelon a desolation: they shall drive out Ashdod at the noon day, and Ekron shall be rooted up" (v. 4).

Did you catch that? One of the warning signs that the day of the Lord is at hand is that Gaza would be forsaken. That is exactly what happened in 2005, when then prime minister Ariel Sharon's Disengagement Plan went into effect and Israeli settlers were forced to evacuate Gaza. It happened on a very significant day on the biblical calendar: at sunset on the ninth of Av—the same day the ten spies had rejected the land during the time of Moses. The Scriptures specifically say that the land of Gaza was given to the tribe of Judah. We may be upset at Sharon for doing this, but it was all a God thing:

> Woe unto the inhabitants of the sea coast, the nation of the Cherethites! the word of the LORD is against you; O Canaan, the land of the Philistines, I will even destroy thee, that there shall be no inhabitant. And the sea coast shall be dwellings and cottages for shepherds, and folds for flocks. And the coast shall be for the remnant of the house of Judah; they shall feed thereupon: in the houses of Ashkelon shall they lie down in the evening: for the LORD their God shall visit them, and turn away their captivity. (Zeph. 2:5–7)

I don't know if it is going to be a tsunami, a meteorite, or what, but God had Gaza evacuated because of the upcoming destruction, only to give it back to Israel after Hamas is destroyed.

Remember Isaiah 26?

Thy *dead men shall live*, together with my dead body shall they arise. Awake and sing, ye that dwell in dust: for thy dew is as the dew of herbs, and the earth shall cast out the dead. Come, my people, enter thou into thy chambers, and shut thy doors about thee: *hide thyself as it were for a little moment*, until the indignation be overpast. For, behold, the LORD cometh out of his place to punish the inhabitants of the earth for their iniquity: the earth also shall disclose her blood, and shall no more cover her slain. (Isa. 26:19–21)

God said He would hide us in the time of trouble.

Many people ask me about my view of when the rapture, or what I really prefer calling the resurrection of the dead, will take place. To be honest, it doesn't matter to me, and I don't waste my time speculating. God isn't consulting my opinion, and He definitely isn't taking a vote on when He should return. Too many people waste their time arguing, and they don't get anything accomplished for the kingdom. But although I have no idea the specific year, I do believe it will happen on the Feast of Trumpets. Israel was protected through the ten plagues of Egypt, Noah was protected during the Flood, and Lot was protected from the destruction of Sodom. So it doesn't matter to me when the Day of the Lord takes place as long as I get the work done that God has asked me to do.

Next, we will see how the wedding of the Messiah is connected to the Feast of Trumpets. It will be quite the celebration all the way through to the Feast of Tabernacles.

Ha Kiddushin/Nesuin (Wedding of the Messiah)

Another part of the Feast of the Trumpets is the marriage ceremony. There is a vivid picture of the wedding ceremony in Joel:

> *Blow the trumpet* in Zion, sanctify a fast, call a solemn assembly: Gather the people, sanctify the congregation, assemble the elders, gather the children, and those that suck the breasts: *let the bridegroom go forth of his chamber, and the bride out of her closet.* (Joel 2:15–16)

The word for closet here is *chuppah*, under which happy couples were married in Jewish weddings. They'd exchange rings, be given seven blessings by the rabbi, and then the groom would break a glass. Finally, the bridegroom would say, "I will go to my father's house and prepare a place for my bride." This place was known as the chamber. We see this picture of preparation in the Gospels:

> Let not your heart be troubled: ye believe in God, believe also in me. In my Father's house are many mansions: if it were not so, I would have told you. *I go to prepare a place for you.* And if I go and prepare a place for you, I will come again, and receive you unto myself; that where I am, there ye may be also. And whither I go ye know, and the way ye know. (John 14:1–4)

When the bridegroom returned, he'd be accompanied by a shout: "Behold, blessed is he who comes in the name of the Lord," and the shofar was blown. This typically was done at night, which is why the lamps were to be kept burning. This is why in Matthew 25 it was important for the virgins to have oil for their lamps: "At midnight there was a cry made, Behold, the bridegroom cometh; go ye out to meet him. Then all those virgins arose, and trimmed their lamps" (vv. 6–7).

The bridegroom would take his bride to the bridal chamber. Afterward would be the marriage supper for all those invited.

The coming of the Messiah is clearly based on the Jewish wedding ceremony in Isaiah:

> For as a young man marrieth a virgin, so shall thy sons marry thee: and *as the bridegroom rejoiceth* over *the bride, so shall thy God rejoice over thee.* I have set watchmen upon thy walls, O Jerusalem, which shall never hold their peace day nor night: ye that make mention of the LORD, keep not silence, And give him no rest, till he establish, and till he make Jerusalem a praise in the earth. (Isa. 62:5–7)

We now come to one of my favorite aspects of the Feast of Trumpets.

HaMelech (Coronation of the Messiah)

One of the aspects of Yom Teruah is to crown God as our King. The sounding of the shofar was to reaffirm God's sovereignty and kingship over the world. It is believed that Adam was created on the day that would become the Feast of Trumpets. Only man, unlike the rest of creation, could properly acknowledge God as sovereign. It was on this day that Adam opened his eyes for the very first time and beheld the wonders of creation.

There are four parts to the enthronement ceremony of a Jewish king:

1. The giving of the decree
2. The taking of the throne
3. The acclamation
4. The pledging of the subjects' allegiance

Psalm 47 is known as the Coronation Psalm, and in it we see the different aspects:

> *O clap your hands*, all ye people; shout unto God with the voice of triumph. For the LORD most high is terrible; he *is a great King* over all the earth. He shall subdue the people under us, and the nations under our feet. He shall choose our inheritance for us, the excellency of Jacob whom he loved. Selah. (vv. 1–4)

Do you want to be at the coronation of the Messiah? Here God will be declared to be the great King over all the earth, and all of creation will respond. It will be an amazing ceremony where the seas will roar and the floods will clap their hands, for the Lord "cometh to judge the earth: with righteousness shall he judge the world, and the people with equity" (Ps. 98:6–9).

I just can't imagine the intensity and how unbelievable this event will be. Words cannot describe it. So the decree will be given and we will hear the applause of creation. The noise will be consistent with the importance of the event.

Back to the Coronation Psalm, in verse 5 we have the *shout and the shofar of Yom Teruah*: "God is gone up *with a shout,* the LORD with the *sound of a trumpet.*" Verses 6–7 tell of the shouting and praising of the King: "Sing praises to God, sing praises: sing praises unto our King, sing praises. For God is the King of all the earth: sing ye praises with understanding." The shouts and praises to God will echo throughout the universe. Again, I just can't imagine all the excitement, the shouting, the singing from all of creation! I believe the stars and whales and crickets will even be joining in.

In verse 8, the King takes His throne: "God reigneth over the heathen: God *sitteth upon the throne* of his holiness." What a ceremony that will be! I'm out of breath just thinking about it. In verse 9, the believers in Yeshua are gathered in His presence, and they all pledge their allegiance: "The *princes of the people are gathered together,* even the people of the God of Abraham: for the shields of the earth belong unto God: he is greatly exalted."

Remember how all the feasts of the Lord are not only divine appointments but also dress rehearsals? At every Feast of Trumpets we celebrate at El Shaddai Ministries, we rehearse the coronation of Yeshua as King over all the earth. We shout and sing praises to the King while shofars are being blown all throughout the congregation. We have two of the best shofar players you have ever heard, and they blow the shofar one hundred times. You can experience the service through live stream from our website. Every year we have churches, home fellowships, and families join us from every time zone around the entire world. People from every tribe, nation, and tongue blow shofars and shout God's praises on the Feast of Trumpets. Beginning at different times across the world, the celebration travels across the globe like the wave you see at baseball games. It's a wave of shofars proclaiming God as King over all the earth. Join us if you can! Remember these are the feasts of the Lord! All too often, due to anti-Semitism, these divine appointments are totally ignored. But if you belong to the Lord, these feasts belong to you.

When you really grasp the significance of this being a dress rehearsal on the appointed day, it will revolutionize your life. In heaven on the very same day, the heavenly hosts are also rehearsing the coming of the Messiah! Can you imagine, on the Feast of Trumpets, here you are, practicing and shouting the praises of God, rehearsing His coming, and some year, on that very day, you will be literally transported right into His presence—you blink, and there you are, joining the heavenly reality!

> Thou shalt arise, and have mercy upon Zion: for the time to favour her, yea, the set time, is come. For thy servants take pleasure in her stones, and favour the dust thereof. So the heathen shall fear the name of the LORD, and all the kings of the earth thy glory. When the LORD shall build up Zion, he shall appear in his glory. (Ps. 102:13–16)

Many people tell me they thought Messiah is supposed to come as a thief in the night. They are correct, but we have to read in context to *whom* He comes as a thief in the night. Let's start with the book of Revelation:

> And unto the angel of the church in Sardis write; These things saith he that hath the seven Spirits of God, and the seven stars; I know thy works, that thou hast a name that thou livest, and *art dead*. Be watchful, and strengthen the things which remain, that are ready to

die: for I have not found thy works perfect before God. Remember therefore how thou hast received and heard, and hold fast, and repent. *If* therefore thou shalt *not watch, I will come on thee as a thief,* and thou shalt not know what hour I will come upon thee. (Rev. 3:1–3)

Here Messiah comes as a thief in the night to the dead church, who is not watching and whose spiritual fire has gone out. In Leviticus, the priests were warned to make sure the fire *never* went out:

Command Aaron and his sons, saying, This is the law of the burnt offering: It is the burnt offering, because of the burning upon the altar *all night* unto the morning, and the fire of the altar shall be burning in it. . . . And the fire on the altar shall be kept burning on it. *It shall not be put out.* And the priest shall burn wood on it every morning, and lay the burnt offering in order on it. And he shall burn on it the fat of the peace offerings. The fire shall ever be burning on the altar; *it shall never go out.* (Lev. 6:9, 12–13)

According to the *Jewish Encyclopedia,* "The captain of the guard saw that every man was alert, chastising a priest if found asleep at his post, and sometimes even punishing him by *burning his shirt upon him,* as a warning to others with fire from the altar he should have been watching!" (Mid. i. 1). Likewise, we are always to be watching.

In a later section of Revelation 3, we read about the church of Laodicea. It was the rich, blind, lukewarm church. Jesus said to them, "Thou sayest, I am rich . . . and knowest not that thou art wretched, and miserable, and poor, and blind, and naked" (Rev. 3:17). The Lord counsels them to buy His gold and His raiment, that they might be rich and clothed and that "the shame of thy *nakedness* do not appear." He also advises, "Anoint thine eyes with eyesalve, that thou mayest see" (v. 18). When we connect this to this next verse, we get the whole picture:

> Behold, I come as a thief. Blessed is he that watcheth, and keepeth his garments, lest he walk *naked, and they see his shame.* (Rev. 16:15)

Wow! The Lord will come as a thief not only to the dead church but also to the wealthy, blind, lukewarm church. Do you go to a dead, lukewarm church that believes the Lord will come as a thief in the night to them? He won't if they get on God's calendar and begin to watch! This book is a call to the church to wake up and watch at the appointed times.

"Well, what about where it says you won't know the day or the hour?" you might ask. First off, we need to look at the context of that verse and see who Jesus is addressing:

> And *the foolish* said unto the wise, Give us of your oil; for our lamps are gone out. But the wise answered, saying, Not so; lest there be not enough for us and you: but go ye rather to them that sell, and buy for yourselves. And while they went to buy, the bridegroom came; and *they that were ready went in with him to the marriage*: and the door was shut. Afterward came also the *other virgins*, saying, Lord, Lord, open to us. But he answered and said, Verily I say unto you, *I know you not.* Watch therefore, for *ye know neither the day nor the hour wherein the Son of man cometh.* (Matt. 25:8–13)

It is to the foolish virgins that the bridegroom says, "I know you not," because they were not watching. To whom else is this comment directed?

In Luke 12:37, Yeshua says, "Blessed are those servants, whom the lord when he cometh *shall find watching.*" Whether He comes in the second watch or the third watch, they who are awake and ready will be blessed (v. 38). The Lord goes on to compare the *un*prepared to a homeowner who's been robbed. "If the goodman of the house had known what hour the thief would come, he would have watched, and not have suffered his house to be broken through." Yeshua then warns, "Be ye therefore ready also: for the Son of man cometh at an hour when ye think not" (vv. 39–40).

After hearing this, Peter asks who the parable is for: just the disciples or for everyone? Well, let's see:

And the Lord said, *Who then is that faithful and wise steward*, whom his lord shall make ruler over his household, to give them their portion of meat in due season? Blessed is that servant, whom his lord when he cometh *shall find so doing.* Of a truth I say unto you, that he will make him ruler over all that he hath. *But and if* that servant say in his heart, My lord delayeth his coming; and shall begin to beat the menservants and maidens, and to eat and drink, and to be drunken; The lord of *that servant will come in a day when he looketh not for him*, and at an hour when he is not aware, and will cut him in sunder, and will appoint him his portion with the unbelievers. (Luke 12:42–46)

So it is the foolish virgins and the evil servants to whom Messiah's coming will be like a thief in the night. His faithful servants will be watching!

Yeshua even rebuked the religious leaders of His day for not watching: "When it is evening, ye say, It will be fair weather: for the sky is red. And in the morning, It will be foul weather to day: for the sky is red and lowering. O ye hypocrites, ye can discern the face of the sky; but can ye not *discern the signs of the times?*" (Matt. 16:3).

So far we've learned that when the Bible mentions seasons, it is not talking about winter and summer but the appointed times. So when we read the following passage, we understand now that Paul is talking about the importance of being on God's calendar.

> But of the *times and* the *seasons*, brethren, ye have no need that I write unto you. For yourselves know perfectly that the day of the *Lord so cometh as a thief in the night.* For when they shall say, Peace and safety; then sudden destruction cometh upon them, as travail upon a woman with child; and they shall not escape. *But ye, brethren, are not in darkness, that that day should overtake you as a thief.* (1 Thess. 5:1–4)

Paul is saying that because they know the appointed times, the Day of the Lord will not come to them as a thief in the night because they know when to be watching! Understand that I am not setting dates. I have no idea what year this will take place. All I am saying is the feast days are the appointed times for the dress rehearsals when the events will take place some year. If you are not aware of when these vital dates fall on our pagan calendar, you will be caught unawares. So how do we avoid that? Keep the commandments of the Lord, know them, love them, and bind them on your heart. Most people don't think of Proverbs as being prophetic, but this is exactly what Proverbs 7 says: "My son, keep my words, and lay up my commandments with thee. Keep my commandments, *and live*; and my *law* [Torah] as the apple of thine eye. Bind them upon thy fingers, write them upon the table of thine heart" (vv. 1–3).

The reason to have the Torah written on your heart is so you will not be deceived in the black and dark night at the end of this age. There is a great harlot loose on the earth. In Revelation 17:5, she is called the "MOTHER OF HARLOTS AND ABOMINATIONS OF THE EARTH." Proverbs 7 continues its warning by alluding to this harlot:

> Say unto wisdom, Thou art my sister; and call understanding thy kinswoman: that they may keep thee from the *strange woman*, from the stranger which *flattereth with her words*. For at the window of my house I looked through my casement, and beheld among the simple ones, I discerned among the youths, a young man void of understanding, passing through the street near her corner; and he went the way to her house, In the twilight, in the evening, *in the black and dark night*: And, behold, there met him *a woman with the attire of an harlot*, and subtle of heart. (Prov. 7:4–10)

Before I finish the prophetic story in Proverbs, I need to lay another foundation at what Yeshua taught was His role. He said that "the Son of man is as a man taking *a far journey, who left his house*, and gave *authority to his servants*, and to every *man his work*, and commanded the porter *to watch*" (Mark 13:34). We know that He left this world and ascended to heaven—a far journey. He also gave authority to His servants, us, and He commanded us to work and to watch, as He will be gone for a while:

> For the kingdom of heaven is as a man *travelling into a far country*, who called his own servants, and delivered unto them his goods. And unto one he gave five talents, to another two, and to another one; to every man according to his several ability; and straightway *took his journey*. (Matt. 25:14–15)

In Matthew 20, Yeshua is likened also to a householder, or "goodman of the house":

> For the kingdom of heaven is like unto a man that is an householder, which went out early in the morning to hire labourers into his vineyard . . . [Some labourers] murmured against the *goodman of the house*. (Matt. 20:1, 11)

With this additional understanding that Yeshua is the goodman of the house, who has given authority and talents to His servants and then taken a long journey, Proverbs 7 becomes more clear. The harlot entices, "Come, let us take our fill of love . . . Let us solace ourselves with loves. For the *goodman* is not at home, he is gone a long journey: He hath taken a bag of money with him, and will come home at *the day appointed*" (vv. 18). The Hebrew word for "day appointed" refers specifically to the Feast of Trumpets on the new moon when the moon is concealed.

The Antichrist, the false prophet, and the harlot all know the appointed times. If only God's people did!

We have seen so far that the feasts of the Lord are appointed times in His day planner; they are dress rehearsals. Now we will examine the importance of letting everybody know.

Acts 3:21 declares that Yeshua is to remain in heaven until the restitution of all things, and one of those things is His calendar to the body of Messiah. Leviticus 23:2 says that God's people are to *proclaim* these important days. The Hebrew word translated as "proclaim" means "to call out by name and bid them to come." We see this in the Gospel of Matthew, where the Master tells his servants to "call them that were bidden" to come to the wedding (22:3). Would you refuse an invitation to the wedding supper of the Messiah? Believe it or not, some will! In the parable, there were many who made light of the feast and "and went their ways, one to his farm, another to his merchandise" (v. 5) There were even some who killed the servants who tried to invite them to the joyful festivity. "But when the king heard thereof, he was wroth: and he sent forth his armies, and destroyed those murderers, and burned up their city" (v. 7). The Master then sent other servants out, again telling them to "go to the highways, and as many as ye shall find, bid to the marriage" (v. 9).

There are some Christians who say the feasts are all done away with. They completely misuse and misunderstand two verses. Remember the Scripture verse in Acts that talks about people who tried to worship Paul and Barnabas, thinking they were the gods of Jupiter and Mercury? The Apostles told them to "*turn from these vanities* unto the living God" (Acts 14:15). Guess where they were geographically when this occurred? They were in Galatia! It was the Galatians who had the problem of worshipping other gods instead of the Creator.

The Galatians believed in astrology, and their calendars were totally based on the horoscope and paganism. Just like in China, where they have the year of the pig or rabbit, these pagans-turned-believers in Galatia went back to observing the solar calendar, not the biblical calendar. Paul admonishes them for holding on to their pagan astrology practices:

> Howbeit then, when ye knew not God, ye did service unto them which by nature are no gods. But now, after that ye have known God, or rather are known of God, how *turn ye again* to the weak and beggarly elements, whereunto ye desire again to be in bondage? Ye *observe days, and months, and times, and years.* I am afraid of you, lest I have bestowed upon you labour in vain. (Gal. 4:8–11)

I'm sure Paul was wondering why in the world they would leave the biblical calendar and go back to the pagan one! All the terms Paul is using here describe the pagan calendar. We know this because in other passages when Paul refers to the biblical calendar, he doesn't use the word *months* but *new moon* and refers not to *days* but *holy days* and *sabbath days.* For instance:

> Let no man therefore judge you . . . in respect of an *holyday, or of the new moon, or of the sabbath days:* which are a shadow of things to come; the body is of Christ. (Col. 2:16–18)

Wow! Do you catch this? The Colossians were the Galatians' next-door neighbors and yet the Colossians kept the holy days. Paul was saying to them not to let the backslidden Galatians judge them, because they are doing exactly the right thing. Then Paul went to describe the feasts as shadows of things *to come.*

Many people are anti-Semites and want to do away with everything Jewish. You can hear it and feel it in their words and tone. They immediately reject anything the Jews say, declaring it to be "rabbinic" or the "traditions of men." Then they turn right around and follow their own man-made traditions. We need to remember Yeshua was Jewish. He was born a Jew, lived as a Jew, died as a Jew, and, to the shock of many, will return to the Jewish homeland to live in Jerusalem, the Eternal Capital!

Let's go now to the next great feast, Yom Kippur, and see its prophetic meaning.

Yom Kippur (Day of Atonement)

Yom Kippur is the holiest day of the year. It was actually known in biblical times as *Yom Kippurim,* which is in the plural, as there were several atonements that had to be made, as seen in Leviticus 16:33: "And he shall make an *atonement for the holy sanctuary,* and he shall make an atonement *for the tabernacle* of the congregation, and *for the altar,* and he shall make an atonement *for the priests,* and *for all the people* of the congregation."

The passage goes on to tell how Aaron would cast lots for two goats. (It was always a good sign when the lot—a coin or type of dice—for the Lord turned up in the right hand of the priest.) The two goats combined made up one offering. One would be sacrificed to the Lord, and the other would become the scapegoat, to be taken out to the Judean wilderness and eventually tossed over a cliff. A scarlet thread was tied around one of the goat's horns, and another tied to the Temple door. If the scarlet thread on the Temple door turned white, the people knew their sins were forgiven.

The Day of Atonement was to be on the tenth day of the seventh month, when all the Israelites were to have a holy dress rehearsal and afflict their souls. It was the most solemn day of the year and was considered a Sabbath of rest. The people would fast for twenty-five hours. When we understand this Jewish custom, we realize that in Acts 27:9, where we are told that "sailing was now dangerous, because *the fast* was now already past," the "fast" Luke referred to was Yom Kippur.

So what happened on the first Yom Kippur after the Israelites left Egypt? In Exodus 32, we read that after Aaron made the golden calf, Moses went up to the mount and fasted for forty days. Historically, he came down on Yom Kippur with the good news that atonement had been made and God wanted to tabernacle among them. That is when they gathered all the material to begin building the tabernacle—at the Feast of Tabernacles! On this holiest day of the year, we have the holiest man (the high priest) going into the holiest place on earth (the holy of holies) to proclaim the holiest name (YHWH).

The whole concept of Yom Kippur was to take away sins. (Of course, at the time, it was the sin of the nation of Israel, not of the Gentiles, that was to be atoned for.) In Psalms 103:12, we are told how far away God wants to cast our sins from us: *"as far as the east is from the west."* Note that he didn't say as far as north is from the south because when you go south long enough, you eventually start going north again, but when you go east, you always go east. This was the day the nation of Israel was to be atoned for. It was not meant for the Gentiles.

According to Leviticus 16, the high priest would take off the royal garments and wear only white linen garments, which symbolize righteousness: "though your sins be as scarlet, they shall be as white as snow" (Isa. 1:18). Imagine having on a white linen garment while you are slaughtering sacrifices!

The Talmud relates four ominous events that took place forty years before the Temple's destruction—and amazingly, about the time of the death of Yeshua:

1. The lot for the Lord's goat would come up in the priest's left hand.

2. The scarlet thread stopped turning white.

3. The westernmost light on the Temple menorah wouldn't stay lit.

4. The Temple doors would open by themselves.[1]

Josephus records in his book *Wars of the Jews* that the Temple door was made of brass and was shut with difficulty by twenty-five men. He goes on to say that the men of learning understood this fourth event to mean that the door was being opened to the advantage of the enemy. They saw a prophetic reference in Zechariah 11:1, which says, "Open thy doors, O Lebanon, that the fire may devour thy cedars."

Since the feasts are dress rehearsals, in Leviticus the

---

1   *Yoma* is the fifth article of the Order of Festivals found in the Talmud. These four events are found in Yoma 4:5b.

Lord outlines very clearly how the service at the feast should take place. Let's compare some descriptions of Yom Kippur found in Leviticus with similar descriptions in Revelation to see if we can find a Yom Kippur service in John's prophecy.

Prayers of the Saints

The Psalmist tells us that our prayers are to "*be set forth before* [God] *as incense*; and the lifting up of [our] hands as the evening sacrifice" (Ps. 141:2). This is what we see in Leviticus:

> And he shall take a *censer full of burning coals of fire from off the altar* before the LORD, and his hands full of sweet incense beaten small, and bring it within the vail: And he shall *put the incense upon the fire before the LORD*, that the cloud of the incense may cover the mercy seat that is upon the testimony, that he die not: And he shall take of the blood of the bullock, and sprinkle it with his finger upon the mercy seat eastward; and before the mercy seat shall he sprinkle of the blood with his finger *seven times*. Then shall he kill the goat of the sin offering, that is for the people, and bring his blood within the vail, and do with that blood as he did with the blood of the bullock, and sprinkle it upon the mercy seat, and before the mercy seat. (Lev. 16:12–15)

So what do we find in Revelation?

> And another angel came and stood at the altar, having a golden censer; and there was given unto him much incense, that he should offer it with the prayers of all saints upon the *golden altar which was before the throne*. And the smoke of the incense, which came with the prayers of the saints, ascended up before God out of the angel's hand. And the angel took the censer, and filled it

with *fire of the altar*, and cast it into the earth: and there were voices, and thunderings, and lightnings, and an earthquake. And the seven angels which had the seven trumpets prepared themselves to sound. (Rev. 8:3–6)

You can't help but see the parallel!

The Holy Ark

We also know that it was only on Yom Kippur that the high priest could go into the Holy of Holies and see the ark of the covenant. Everything on earth was to be patterned after the Temple in heaven, so what do we find there?

And the nations were angry, and thy wrath is come, and the time of the dead, that they should be judged, and that thou shouldest give reward unto thy servants the prophets, and to the saints, and them that fear thy name, small and great; and shouldest destroy them which destroy the earth. And the temple of God was opened in heaven, and there was seen in his temple the *ark of his testament*: and there were lightnings, and voices, and thunderings, and an earthquake, and great hail. (Rev. 11:18–19)

Yom Kippur is judgment day! The court is in session and the books are opened on Rosh Hashana, but on Yom Kippur the books are closed and the sentence is meted out.

The Harvest

God wanted to keep things simple for us, so He used concepts we would be familiar with. The spring feasts were around the barley and wheat harvest. The fall feasts were around the grape harvest. In Acts we read that during the wheat harvest at Shavuot, three thousand souls were harvested into the kingdom. In Matthew we see that the fall feasts will be the same way: "The field is the world; the good seed are the children of the kingdom; but the tares are the children of the wicked one; the enemy that sowed them is the devil; the harvest is the end of the world; and the reapers are the angels" (13:38–39).

In Revelation we read: "And another angel came out from the altar, which had power over fire; and cried with a loud cry to him that had the sharp sickle, saying, Thrust in thy sharp sickle, and *gather the clusters of the vine of the earth; for her grapes* are fully ripe" (14:18). Here, grapes are mentioned because just as the spring feasts were fulfilled in springtime the fall feasts will be fulfilled in the fall, when grapes are harvested.

A Holy Tabernacle

Look at this next connection between the Yom Kippur service in Leviticus and Revelation. Leviticus 16 says:

> And he shall make an atonement for the holy place, because of the uncleanness of the children of Israel, and because of their transgressions in all their sins: and so shall he do for the tabernacle of the congregation, that remaineth among them in the midst of their uncleanness. And there shall *be no man in the tabernacle* of the congregation when he goeth in to make an atonement in the holy place, until he come out, and have made an *atonement for himself, and for his household, and for all the congregation of Israel.* (vv. 16–17)

This holy day was specifically for *Israel*, and no one else was allowed into the tabernacle.

Now, in Revelation 15:8 we read:

> And the temple was filled with smoke from the glory of God, and from his power; and *no man was able to enter into the temple*, till the *seven plagues* of the *seven angels* were fulfilled.

A Day of Vengeance

Yom Kippur is the day of vengeance on God's adversaries, and God Himself is the blood avenger. On Yom Kippur everyone comes dressed in white. The high priests' white garments are splattered with the blood of the sacrifices. With this in mind, take a look at these verses:

> For true and righteous are his judgments: for he hath judged the great whore, which did corrupt the earth with her fornication, and hath *avenged the blood of his servants* at her hand . . . And he was clothed with *a vesture dipped in blood*: and his name is called The Word of God. And the armies which were in heaven followed him upon white horses, *clothed in fine linen, white and clean.* And out of his mouth goeth a sharp sword, that with it he should smite the nations: and he shall rule them with a rod of iron: and he *treadeth the winepress* of the fierceness and wrath of Almighty God. (Rev. 19:2, 13–15)

I believe this is telling us that this event will happen some year on Yom Kippur!

Removing the Veil

Yom Kippur was all about removing the veil that hides God from humanity. It was the only day the high priest could speak to God "face to face." We see a future Yom Kippur event happening for the Jewish people in Ezekiel 20: "As I live, saith the Lord GOD, surely with a mighty hand, and with a stretched out arm, and with fury poured out, will I rule over you: And I will bring you out from the people, and will gather you out of the countries wherein ye are scattered, with a mighty hand, and with a stretched out arm, and with fury poured out. And I will bring you into the wilderness of the people, and *there will I plead with you face to face*" (vv. 33–35).

Yom Kippur is amazing in that it is the one day every year when the Israelites seek God's face. It is the one time of the year when the veil is removed and Israel will some day realize Yeshua is the Messiah. These verses in Hosea, in which God is speaking to Ephraim and Judah, are incredible:

For I will be unto Ephraim as a lion, and as a young lion to the house of Judah: I, even I, *will tear and go away*; I will take away, and none shall rescue him. *I will go and return to my place*, till they acknowledge their offence, and *seek my face: in their affliction* they will seek me early.

Come, and let us return unto the LORD: for he hath torn, and he will heal us; he hath smitten, and he will bind us up. After *two days* will he revive us: in the *third day he will raise us up*, and we shall live in his sight. Then shall we know, if we follow on to know the LORD: his going forth is prepared as the morning; and he shall come unto us as the rain, as the latter and former rain unto the earth. (Hos. 5:14–6:3)

This is exactly what happened. In AD 70, the Temple was destroyed. Yeshua then returned to heaven. We know that "one day is with the Lord as a thousand years" (2 Peter 3:8). So after two days, or two thousand years, Israel is restored. Now we are on the verge of the third day, or millennial reign, known as the Sabbath rest for one thousand years. This is when the resurrection of the dead will occur, God will raise us up, and we will live in His sight! Hallelujah!

The veil is spread over the non-Jews too. Isaiah 25:7 says it "is spread over all nations." We read in the New Testament that even believers in Yeshua don't see clearly: "For now *we see through a glass, darkly*; but then face to face: now I know *in part*" (1 Cor. 13:12). This is again Yom Kippur terminology, and some year, when the veil is removed from the Gentiles and "in *the day of affliction*, the Gentiles shall come unto [God] from the ends of the earth, and shall say, Surely our fathers have inherited lies, vanity, and things wherein there is no profit" (Jer. 16:19).

As Christians we know we see through a glass darkly and only know in part. But too often Christians think the Jews are totally blinded. That is completely untrue. Sure, God declared in Isaiah that they would be blinded, but their blindness was only partial as well:

> For I would not, brethren, that ye should be ignorant of this mystery, lest ye should be wise in your own conceits; that *blindness in part is happened to Israel*, until the fulness of the Gentiles be come in. And *so all Israel shall be saved*: as it is written, There shall come out of Sion the Deliverer, and *shall turn away ungodliness from Jacob: For this is my covenant unto them, when I shall take away their sins.* As concerning the gospel, they are enemies for your

sakes: *but as touching the election, they are beloved for the fathers' sakes. For the gifts and calling of God are without repentance.* (Rom. 11:25–29)

So Jews and Christians both are partially blinded— the Jews concerning the Messiah, and the Christians concerning the relevance of the Torah. Christians need to realize there is only one tree—Israel. We are grafted into that tree, into Israel, to whom all the promises of God belong. Too many people erroneously judge the Jewish people. They put upon all the Jewish people for all history the guilt of what a few thugs did two thousand years ago. However, God declared that no matter what the Jewish people do, He will always be in covenant with them:

> And they shall teach no more every man his neighbour, and every man his brother, saying, Know the LORD: for they shall all know me, from the least of them unto the greatest of them, saith the LORD: for *I will forgive their iniquity,* and *I will remember their sin no more.* Thus saith the LORD, which giveth the sun for a light by day, and the ordinances of the moon and of the stars for a light by night, which divideth the sea when the waves thereof roar; the LORD of hosts is his name: *If those ordinances depart from before me, saith the LORD, then the seed of Israel also shall cease from being a nation* before me forever. Thus saith the LORD; *If heaven above can be measured, and the foundations of the earth searched out beneath, I will also cast off all the seed of Israel for all that they have done, saith the LORD.* (Jer. 31:34–36)

Some people ask me, "Why don't the Jewish people see Jesus as the suffering servant Messiah?" To answer that question, let's begin with Genesis when Joseph's brothers went to Egypt to buy food from the brother whom they'd sold into slavery. "Joseph knew his brethren, but they knew not him" (Gen. 42:8). The reason Joseph's brothers did not recognize him was because he looked, smelled, and was dressed like an Egyptian, and not a Jew. Sadly, since the days of the early church, we have been presenting to the Jew a "Jesus" in Egyptian clothes! Jesus is seen as a white (sometimes even blond!) European, far from His own roots! Thing is, His name wasn't even Jesus.[1] Talk about identity theft. His name is Yeshua. This is akin to what happened during the Holocaust, when Jewish children were turned over to Gentiles for protection. After the war, when Jewish parents tried to find their lost loved ones, they were told that no Jewish children were around. This lie was based on the non-Jews' view that since they had converted these Jewish children to Christianity, the children were no longer Jews. As a result, their poor relatives could not be reconnected to them. We need to return Yeshua to His own family.

Jacob's sons knew they were "verily guilty concerning [their] brother, in that [they] saw the anguish of his soul" (Gen. 42:21). It wasn't until Judah repented and took responsibility for the sale of Joseph that Joseph revealed himself:

---

1   *Jesus* is a totally manufactured name. It is a distorted transliteration of the original Greek into Latin, and then into the various evolutions of the English language.

Then Joseph could not refrain himself before all them that stood by him; and he cried, Cause every man to go out from me. And there *stood no man with him,* while *Joseph made himself known unto his brethren.* And he wept aloud: *and the Egyptians and the house of Pharaoh heard.* And Joseph said unto his brethren, I am Joseph; doth my father yet live? And his brethren could not answer him; for *they were troubled at his presence.* And Joseph said unto his brethren, Come near to me, I pray you. And they came near. And he said, I am Joseph your brother, whom ye sold into Egypt. Now therefore be not grieved, nor angry with yourselves, that ye sold me hither: for God did send me *before you to preserve life.* (Gen. 45:1–6)

Did you notice that "there stood no man with him" when he made himself known? Sounds like a Yom Kippur event to me. They were troubled at his presence. The good news was that it was all God's plan to begin with! The Jewish people were just as surprised that Joseph was Jewish as the Gentiles were. I think it will come as just as big a surprise when the church realizes Yeshua is still Jewish!

Another reason Jews don't think Yeshua could be the Messiah is because they believe that He threw out the Torah (which most of Christianity teaches), and if He threw out the Torah, then He is a false prophet. When it comes to deciding if a prophet is a true prophet or not, most people think a prophet is true if what he says comes to pass. But that is not the true litmus test. Yes, Yeshua was a prophet who did many signs and wonders and miracles, and what He said would happen did come to pass, but that is not enough. Most Christians believe the Torah to be the Word of God.

If that is the case, let's read from Deuteronomy, the book most often quoted by Yeshua:

> If there arise among you a prophet, or a dreamer of dreams, and giveth thee a sign or a wonder, and the sign or the wonder come to pass, whereof he spake unto thee, saying, Let us go after other gods, which thou hast not known, and let us serve them; thou shalt not hearken unto the words of that prophet, or that dreamer of dreams: for the LORD your God proveth you, to know whether ye love the LORD your God with all your heart and with all your soul. Ye shall walk after the LORD your God, and fear him, and keep his commandments, and obey his voice, and ye shall serve him, and cleave unto him. (Deut. 13:1–4)

Basically what this is saying is that the true prophet will not cause you to serve other gods, but he will truly love the Lord God's commandments rather than some man's commandments or tradition. So even though Yeshua did a lot of wonderful things, if He did not keep the Lord's commandments, He cannot be the Messiah.

Yeshua never did away with any of the Torah. He did not "come to destroy the law, or the prophets" but to fulfill it. "Till heaven and earth pass," He said, "one jot or one tittle shall in no wise pass from the law, till all be fulfilled" (Matt. 5:17–18).

These are powerful words from the Master. Maybe there's been a veil over our eyes.

Feast of Tabernacles / Sukkot / Booths / Feast of Nations / Feast of Ingathering

This has to be my favorite appointed time. You will soon

discover why. But first I want to make a point. You want to celebrate your birthday on your birthday, your anniversary on your anniversary. How would you feel if your spouse said, "We don't need to celebrate your birthday or our anniversary, because every day is your birthday and every day is our anniversary"? Keep this in mind as we continue to mine the truths of these feast days.

So now let's look at our final feast, the Feast of Tabernacles. In Leviticus, Moses spells out the rules for this festival: "And ye shall keep it a feast unto the LORD seven days in the year. It shall be a statute forever in your generations: ye shall celebrate it in the seventh month. Ye shall *dwell in booths* seven days; all that are Israelites born shall *dwell in booths*: That your generations may know that I made the children of Israel to *dwell in booths*, when I brought them out of the land of Egypt: I am the LORD your God" (Lev. 23:41–43).

The Hebrew word for "booths" is *sukkot*, which means "huts," "tabernacles," or "tents." In Genesis, Jacob, journeyed to a particular town and made booths, or sukkot, for his cattle there. So the town became known as Sukkot.

In Deuteronomy, we see that the Feast of Tabernacles was one of three pilgrimage festivals, during which all the males twenty years and older were required to go to Jerusalem: "Three times in a year shall all thy males appear before the LORD thy God in the place which he shall choose; in the feast of unleavened bread, and in the feast of weeks, and in the *feast of tabernacles*" (Deut. 16:16).

Ever since the fall of Adam and Eve, God's ultimate plan has always been to dwell, or tabernacle, among His people. It was on the first Feast of Tabernacles that Israel, while in the wilderness, began building God's tabernacle so He could dwell with them (Ex. 35). Zechariah, quoting the Lord, prophesied that Yeshua, "the man whose name is The BRANCH," would come from Israel and would "build the temple of the LORD" (Zech. 6:12). In spite of the fact that the Holy Temple in Jerusalem was destroyed twice, God will still achieve His goal of dwelling with us. This will happen after an epic battle that is coming over Jerusalem when the feet of the Lord will land on the Mount of Olives.

> Then shall the LORD go forth, and fight against those nations, as when he fought in the day of battle. *And his feet shall stand in that day upon the mount of Olives*, which is before Jerusalem on the east, and the mount of Olives shall cleave in the midst thereof. . . . And it shall come to pass, that every one that is left of all the nations which came against Jerusalem shall even go up from year to year to worship the King, the LORD of hosts, and *to keep the feast of tabernacles*. And it shall be, that whoso will not come up of all the families of the earth unto Jerusalem to worship the King, the LORD of hosts, even upon them shall be no rain. And if the family of Egypt go not up, and come not, that have no rain; there *shall be the plague*, wherewith the LORD will smite the heathen that come not up to *keep the feast of tabernacles*. This shall be the punishment of Egypt, and the punishment of all nations that come not up to *keep the feast of tabernacles*. (Zech. 14:3–4, 16–19)

This event obviously has not happened yet. Three times the passage declares that all nations will come to Jerusalem to keep the Feast of Tabernacles. We might as well start practicing now! Again, if the Lord is the same yesterday, today, and forever, would He say that the Feast of Tabernacles is good, then it's bad, and then it's good again and ask all nations to keep it again? After a thousand years of rest, there will be a new heaven and a new earth, and the tabernacle of God will be with men. "*He will dwell with them*, and they shall be his people, and God himself shall be with them, and be their God" (Rev. 21:3).

A major aspect of this feast is God's desire for us to realize that this earth and our bodies are only "tabernacles," or temporary dwelling places:

> Lift up your eyes to the heavens, and look upon the earth beneath: for the heavens shall vanish away like smoke, and the earth shall wax old like a garment, and they that dwell therein shall die in like manner. (Isa. 51:6)

> For we know that if our earthly house of this tabernacle were dissolved, we have a building of God, an house not made with hands, eternal in the heavens. (2 Cor. 5:1)

Peter, facing his demise, recognized that his body was a temporary dwelling when he said, "Shortly I must put off this *my tabernacle*, even as our Lord Jesus Christ hath showed me" (2 Peter 1:14). He went on to affirm to his readers that "the power and coming" of the Lord Jesus Christ was not a fable but that he and the other apostles were "eyewitnesses of his majesty" (v. 16). When did Peter see the power and coming of the Messiah? We read about it in the Gospel of Mark, where he was allowed to see into the future:

And [Jesus] said unto them, Verily I say unto you, That there be some of them that stand here, which shall not taste of death, till they have seen the *kingdom of God come with power*. And after six days Jesus taketh with him Peter, and James, and John, and leadeth them up into an high mountain apart by themselves: and he was transfigured before them. . . . And Peter answered and said to Jesus, Master, it is good for us to be here: and let us make *three tabernacles*; one for thee, and one for Moses, and one for Elias. (Mark 9:1–2, 5)

Why would Peter want to build three tabernacles? It is because he saw this event happening during the Feast of Tabernacles!

The Feast of Tabernacles was to be a time of great joy because it was a celebration of God's "tabernacling" among His people. According to Josephus, more than two million people were in Jerusalem for the festivals during his time.

During the feast, which mainly took place in the Women's Court, the Levites played music. As the people sang, the men would dance before them while juggling flaming torches. The Levites, standing on the fifteen steps that ascend from the Women's Court to the Court of Israel, played on lyres, harps, trumpets, and many other instruments. Two priests would blow silver trumpets at the top of the stairs on either side of the entrance to the great gate of the Court. All this was done to honor the commandment of the water libation, which was based on oral tradition.

In the Women's Court there were four enormous candlesticks with four golden bowls at the top of each. They were seventy-five feet high. Worn-out priestly garments that had been stained from the priest's duties at the sacrificial altar were used for the wicks. These garments would be cut into strips and kept in the Women's Court. Four young priests-in-training would climb to the top, carrying immense jugs filled with oil that they would then pour into the bowls. The light that emanated from these enormous candles filled every courtyard in Jerusalem. It was during this very feast that Yeshua proclaimed himself to be the light of the world: "Then spake Jesus again unto them, saying, *I am the light of the world*: he that followeth me shall not walk in darkness, but shall have the light of life" (John 8:12).

So many people were at the festival that all the priests were on duty for the entire week. The priests were divided into three groups. The first group was responsible for the slaying of all the sacrifices. The second group, headed by the high priest, would go out the Water Gate to the pool of Siloam. The high priest would draw water, known as living water, using a golden vase. Then the multitude would ascend again to the Temple and bring the vessel up to the altar. The priest would pour out the living water on the altar. Another priest poured out wine from a silver pitcher. This ceremony of the water libation was connected to the rainfall. The people would pray for rain and blessings upon the earth for its produce for the coming year. The Psalms was their hymnal, and they would sing specifically from Psalms 118 during the feast of Tabernacles.

The LORD is my strength and song, and is become my salvation. The voice of rejoicing and salvation is in the tabernacles of the righteous: the right hand of the LORD doeth valiantly. (Ps. 118:14–15)

On the seventh day, the last day of the feast, the people would do a "Jericho march" around the altar seven times and then do the water libation while singing. When you understand the ceremony of the feast, it makes Jesus's words about coming to Him for living water much more significant:

> Now the Jews' *feast of tabernacles* was at hand. . . . Now about the midst of *the feast* Jesus went up into the temple, and taught. . . . *In the last day, that great day of the feast*, Jesus stood and cried, saying, If any man thirst, let him come unto me, and drink. He that believeth on me, *as the scripture hath said*, out of *his belly shall flow rivers of living water*. (John 7:2, 14, 37–38)

It was during the time of the festival when the people were singing, "With joy shall ye *draw water out of the wells of salvation*" (Isa. 12:3) that Yeshua cried out to the people to "come unto [Him] and drink." The Hebrew word for salvation is *Yeshua*, so they would have been saying, "With joy shall ye *draw water out of the wells of Yeshua*." This is why He cried out; He was referring to what they had just sung. And right after this the people would have continued singing, "Cry out and shout, thou inhabitant of Zion: for great is the Holy One of Israel in the midst of thee" (Isa. 12:6).

This is just too incredible!

The third group of priests went out the Beautiful Gate over to the Motzah Valley and cut willow branches twenty-five to thirty feet in length. As if in a parade, they'd form rows and rows of priests waving the branches thirty feet apart. You can almost hear the rustling of the wind as it passed through the hundreds of willow branches being waved as the priests ascended to the Temple. The Hebrew word for wind is *ruach,* which can also be translated as "spirit." So here we have the high priest with the living water and his assistant with the wine symbolically representing the blood marching up to the Water Gate on the southern side at the same time the other priests were ascending with willows. This was to be symbolic of the Spirit of God coming upon Jerusalem. Once they arrived at their gates, a priest known as the "pierced one" played a flute calling for the wind and water to enter the Temple.

Because of the commandment to dwell in booths for this feast, there would be thousands of sukkahs dotting the hillside for miles around the city! When John wrote, "the Word was made flesh, and *dwelt among us*" (John 1:14) he used the Greek word *skenoo,* which means "to tent or encamp." So Yeshua was literally camping among the people when He proclaimed Himself to be the Living Waters. Amazing!

We know that the tabernacle built in the wilderness had its beginning at the Feast of Tabernacles. Well, I'm going to prove to you from your own Bible that Messiah's birth was also on the Feast of Tabernacles in late September or early October. We need to begin with the birth of Yochanan the Immerser, better known as John the Baptist:

> There was in the days of Herod, the king of Judaea, a certain priest named *Zacharias,* of the *course of Abia*: and his wife was of the daughters of Aaron, and her name was Elisabeth. . . . And it came to pass, that while he *executed the priest's office* before God *in the order of his course, according to the custom of the priest's office,* his lot

was to burn incense when he went into the temple of the Lord. (Luke 1:5, 8–9)

The priests were divided into courses, or groups, that were named after Aaron's sons, and each had different responsibilities. First Chronicles 24 gives us a picture of how they were divided:

> Now *these are the divisions* of the sons of Aaron. The sons of Aaron; Nadab, and Abihu, Eleazar, and Ithamar. But Nadab and Abihu died before their father, and had no children: therefore Eleazar and Ithamar *executed the priest's office.* . . . The seventh to Hakkoz, *the eighth to Abijah,* . . . *These were the orderings* of them in their service to come into the house of the LORD, *according to their manner.* (vv. 1–2, 10, 19)

There were twenty-four courses of priests, with each course serving twice a year for one week at a time. Three weeks a year during the pilgrimage feasts, all courses would serve due to the multitude of people. The religious year began at the first of Nisan, two weeks before Passover. For simplicity's sake, since it can happen at this time, let's say it is our April 1. Since the Abijah course was the eighth, they would have served the eighth week. This would have been two months from April 1, or June 1. But because all the priests would serve during Passover week, the eighth course actually served during the ninth week, or the second week of our June. But guess what? This takes us to the Feast of Shavuot, or Pentecost, when there would be a huge multitude of people attending this mandatory pilgrimage feast.

This is why it says in Luke: "And *the whole multitude* of the people were praying without at the time of incense. And there appeared unto him an angel of the Lord standing on the right side of the altar of incense" (Luke 1:10–11).

So Zacharias had to serve two weeks in a row: the week of Shavuot and the week for his own course. And "*as soon as* the days of his ministration were accomplished, he departed to his own house. And after those days his wife Elisabeth conceived, and hid herself *five months*" (Luke 1:23–24). This means it was the middle of June when Zacharias went home and his wife conceived. Her five months of hiding takes us from the middle of June to the middle of November. One month later, or the middle of December, an angel appears to Mary:

> And in the *sixth month* the angel Gabriel was sent from God unto a city of Galilee, named Nazareth, . . . And the angel . . . said unto her, The Holy Ghost shall come upon thee, and the power of the Highest shall over-shadow thee: therefore also that holy thing which shall be born of thee shall be called the Son of God. And, behold, thy cousin Elisabeth, she hath also conceived a son in her old age: and this is the *sixth month with her,* who was called barren. (Luke 1:26, 35–36)

So Yeshua is conceived the middle to the end of December, or during Chanukah! Since it was the sixth month for Elizabeth, "Mary abode with her about *three months,* and returned to her own house" (Luke 1:56). It just so happens three months after Chanukah takes you right to Passover, when John was born at the appointed time! And if you add nine months for Mary from the end of December, it takes you to the end of September, putting Yeshua's birth right at the Feast of Tabernacles! Luke 2:6–7 says:

> And so it was, that, while they were there, the days were accomplished that she should be delivered. And she brought forth her firstborn son, and wrapped him in *swaddling clothes*, and laid him in a *manger*; because there was *no room for them in the inn*.

Why was there no room in the inn? Because there were more than two million Jews there for the feasts during the seventh month; that's why. Also, if Yeshua were born in the middle of the winter instead of the seventh month, there would be no shepherds abiding in the fields at that time. And we clearly see from Luke's account that there were shepherds in the field when Yeshua was born:

> And there were in the same country *shepherds abiding in the field*, keeping watch over their flock by night. And, lo, the angel of the Lord came upon them, and the glory of the Lord shone round about them: and they were sore afraid. And the angel said unto them, Fear not: for, behold, I bring you *good tidings of great joy*, which shall be to all people. For unto you is born *this day* in the city of David *a Saviour*, which is Christ the Lord. (Luke 2:8–11)

Israel was commanded to rejoice during this feast, as it was to be a time of great joy. What greater joy could there be than God wanting to tabernacle among us? God was planning His Son's birthday party. He said, "There will be a party on My Son's birthday, and you will sing and rejoice!"

And what are the people singing this first day of the feast?

> The LORD is my strength and song, and is *become my salvation* [Yeshua]. The voice of *rejoicing* and *salvation* [Yeshua] *is in the tabernacles* of the righteous: the right hand of the LORD doeth valiantly. . . . I will praise thee: for thou hast heard me, and art become my salvation [Yeshua]. . . . . *This is the day* which the LORD hath made; *we will rejoice* and *be glad* in it. *Save now,* I beseech thee, O LORD. (Ps. 118:14–15, 21, 24–25)

This is all too wonderful for me as I contemplate the perfect timing of the Almighty. Even the heavenly host joined in on the celebrations going on in the Temple, as "suddenly there was with the angel a multitude of the *heavenly host praising God,* and saying, Glory to God in the highest, and on earth peace, good will toward men" (Luke 2:13–14).

This feast was seven days long, followed by a special eighth day known as Shemini Atzeret, when Israel had "a solemn assembly" (Num. 29:35) and prayed for rain. The eight day is also the day when every "man child among you *shall be circumcised*" (Gen. 17:10). So "when *eight days were accomplished for the circumcising* of the child, his name was called JESUS [Yeshua], which was so named of the angel before he was conceived in the womb" (Luke 2:21). So on this very special day, Yeshua shed His blood through circumcision confirming the covenant of Abraham. Then,

> when the days of her purification *according to the law of Moses* were accomplished, they brought him to Jerusalem, to present him to the Lord; (as it is written in the law of the Lord, Every male that openeth the womb

shall be called holy to the Lord;) and to offer a sacrifice according to that which is said in *the law of the Lord, A pair of turtledoves, or two young pigeons.* (Luke 2:22–24)

Let's go to the Torah to find the complete picture, since it says the purification was done according to the Law:

And when the days of her purifying are fulfilled, for a son, or for a daughter, she shall bring a *lamb of the first year* for a burnt offering, *and a young pigeon, or a turtledove,* for a sin offering, unto the door of the tabernacle of the congregation, unto the priest . . . And *if she be not able to bring a lamb, then she shall bring two turtles, or two young pigeons*; the one for the burnt offering, and the other for a sin offering. (Lev 12:6, 8)

We find that in reality Mary was to offer a lamb and a bird. This tells us that a month after the birth, she still could not afford a lamb, so the magi had not arrived yet! While she and Joseph may have felt a little dismayed at not being able to afford a lamb, little did they know they *had* a lamb—the Lamb of God!

Now fast-forward a couple of millennia. We are living in the last days, but there are prophecies not yet fulfilled. Isaiah says:

In the last days, that the mountain of the LORD's house shall be established in the top of the mountains, and shall be exalted above the hills; and *all nations* shall flow unto it. And many people shall go and say, Come ye, and let us go up to the mountain of the LORD, to the house of the God of Jacob; and *he will teach us* of his ways, and we will walk in his paths: for out of Zion *shall go forth the law* [Torah]*, and the word of the* LORD *from Jerusalem.* And he shall judge among the nations, and shall rebuke many people: and they shall beat their swords into plowshares, and their spears into pruninghooks: nation shall not lift up sword against nation, neither shall they learn war any more. O house of Jacob, come ye, and let us walk in the light of the LORD. (Isa. 2:1–5)

All nations will come to Jerusalem to learn the Torah during the millennial reign. If God is truly the same yesterday, today, and forever, He won't say the Torah was good, now it is bad, and later it will be good again. We need a better perspective of what the Torah really means. Sukkot was given to us by God to instruct us regarding what life would be like during the Messianic Age, when the knowledge of the Messiah and the Spirit of God will cover the earth as the waters cover the sea.

My people are destroyed for lack of knowledge: because thou hast rejected knowledge, I will also reject thee, that thou shalt be no priest to me: seeing thou hast forgotten the law [Torah] of thy God, I will also forget thy children.

5
GOD'S CALENDAR DAYS AND YEARS

any people were freaking out in 2012 when the Mayan calendar ended. They thought it marked the end of time. Of course, the world didn't end, and the reason why is that everyone has been looking at all the wrong calendars. The magi in the Scriptures, who were looking for that famous star in the East, understood something that has been overlooked by all the theologians for more than two thousand years. They understood which one was the right calendar! The reason astronomers can look for mathematical patterns in the heavens is because the Creator is the greatest mathematician in the universe and created everything according to science. It was when I discovered the linking of the eclipses to the biblical calendar in 2008 that everything changed for me. You can watch the teaching of the discovery in the El Shaddai archives. (See the resources section on page 176 for more information.) It all became clear when I simply looked at celestial events in connection to the feasts of the Lord as they happened on the biblical calendar. We need to be on God's timetable!

I used to live in Garden City, Kansas, where the time zone changed from Central Time to Mountain Time. The people who lived in one time zone and worked in another had to have two clocks. When you wanted to call someone in Kansas, you had to make sure you knew whose time zone you should go by. The same situation applies to us. Of course, we need to go by our solar calendar because we live and work in this world. But we also need to follow the calendar God is using when He wants to communicate with us.

JEWISH MONTH	#	LENGTH	GREGORIAN MONTH
NISAN	1	30 DAYS	MARCH–APRIL
IYAR	2	29 DAYS	APRIL–MAY
SIVAN	3	30 DAYS	MAY–JUNE
TAMMUZ	4	29 DAYS	JUNE–JULY
AV	5	30 DAYS	JULY–AUG
ELUL	6	29 DAYS	AUG–SEPT
TISHRI	7	30 DAYS	SEPT–OCT
CHESHVAN	8	29 OR 30 DAYS	OCT–NOV
KISLEV	9	30 OR 29 DAYS	NOV–DEC
TEVET	10	29 DAYS	DEC–JAN
SHEVAT	11	30 DAYS	JAN–FEB
ADAR I	12	30 DAYS	FEB–MARCH
ADAR II	13	30 DAYS	FEB–MARCH

We read that God declared that the sun and the moon were to determine the days and years. What days and years is He talking about? Again, in our Western mind-set, we typically believe it has to do with our calendar, but our calendar, once known as the Julian calendar, was created by a pagan Roman ruler. It is totally based on the sun. This is why we have leap years adding one day every four years. Then along came Pope Gregory, who made a few modifications, and it became known as the Gregorian calendar. It is a very accurate and nice calendar, but it is not the one the God of Abraham, Isaac, and Jacob uses!

The Muslim calendar is based totally on the moon, which is why Ramadan rotates among the different months of the year. But it, too, is not the one that the God of Abraham, Isaac, and Jacob uses. Only the calendar that God spelled out in Genesis is the one that He uses, and according to Genesis it is based on both the sun and the moon! This is why in the Hebrew calendar, the Jews add leap months seven times over nineteen years. When God said He was going to use the sun and moon for days and years, He was referring to the biblical holy days, Jubilee years, and *shemittah* years, which were every seventh year when the land in Israel was to rest or remain fallow. One of the main reasons why the Jewish people went into captivity twenty-six hundred years ago was because they did not observe the shemittah year. Every fiftieth year was the year of Jubilee. The captives were set free, all debts were forgiven, and all land was returned to the previous owners.

We have clearly seen that God specifically created the sun, moon, and stars to send signals to His children at His appointed times on His calendar so we would be aware of when He wants to meet with us. He also wanted to let us know that significant events may be unfolding when heavenly signs fall on those feast days! Why else would Joel, Isaiah, and John (in the book of Revelation), as well as

Yeshua Himself in the Gospels, declare that there would be signs in the sun and the moon and the stars? Because that's why God created them!

Let's look at the added dimension of the significance of when eclipses fall on the Lord's feast days and during special years. To have a complete understanding of biblical prophecy, you need to return to the biblical calendar. Do you remember what Yeshua said to the religious leaders in His day? He called them hypocrites and said that they could "discern the face of the sky and of the earth" but could not "discern this time" (Luke 12:56). And look at what God declared in the book of Jeremiah:

> Yea, the stork in the heaven knoweth *her appointed times;* and the turtle and the crane and the swallow observe the time of their coming; *but my people know not* the judgment of the LORD. (Jer. 8:7)

The birds know their own appointed times but God's people don't know theirs? Notice He is not saying that the unbelievers are unaware, but that His own people are unaware! If you consider yourself a student of prophecy and are not on God's calendar, then you are like a ship in the middle of the ocean without any navigational equipment. Let me give you a perfect example. If you want to know why you need to be on God's calendar to understand prophecy, look at Zechariah:

> Thus saith the LORD of hosts; The *fast of the fourth month,* and the *fast of the fifth,* and the *fast of the seventh,* and the *fast of the tenth, shall be* to the house of Judah *joy*

and gladness, and cheerful feasts; therefore love the truth and peace. (Zech. 8:19)

If you are scratching your head and wondering what this has to do with you or anything today, then you prove my point. These are four specific dates on God's calendar that are days of mourning and fasting, all relating to the destruction of the Temple by Nebuchadnezzar in 587 BC. Zechariah prophesied that these days will be turned from mourning into days of joy. Well, this prophecy has not been fulfilled yet. If you don't know the history, the context, or the days when they fall on our pagan calendar, then you will never know the biblical significance of the prophecy, or when it is fulfilled!

Imagine the Israelis withstanding an invasion or winning a war on one of those very days. Only they would know that a profound biblical prophecy was just fulfilled. The Christian world would be clueless. One of the days mentioned in Zechariah 8:19 refers to the destruction of the Temple on the ninth day of the month of Av. This usually falls on our calendar around late July or early August. Every year, for twenty-five hundred years, the Jewish people have mourned the destruction of the Temple on this day of the biblical calendar. If you don't follow the biblical calendar, then you won't make the connection when this day is at last turned into a day of joy.

Let me expand on this. Do you remember when the ten spies brought the bad report, and therefore the nation of Israel had to wander for forty years in the desert? This happened on the ninth of Av. That is why this day has been cursed throughout history for the Jewish people. In 587 BC, the Temple was destroyed on the ninth of Av. In AD 70, the Romans destroyed the Temple on the ninth of Av. All the Jews were kicked out of England in 1290 on the ninth of Av. They were kicked out of Spain in 1492 on the ninth of Av. World War I started on the ninth of Av. Hitler's proclamation to exterminate all the Jews was also on the ninth of Av. And believe it or not, in 2005, when Israel again rejected the Promised Land and all the Jews were expelled from the Gaza Strip, it was at sunset on the ninth of Av. Most were totally clueless to the significance of this event. The Lebanon war in 2007 started on one of these fast days as well: the seventeenth of Tammuz. It just so happens this is the very day the Israelites worshipped the golden calf at the base of Mount Sinai!

So where did we all go wrong? For that we need to take a look at a little bit of biblical history. It begins with what is called replacement theology, which we touched on briefly in chapter 1. Adherents of this view believe they have replaced the Jews in God's eyes. Replacement theology teaches that the Jews get to keep all the curses and the "church" gets all the blessings. It may come as a surprise to most readers that this began very early in the first century.

Did you know the early church kicked the apostle John and all the Jews out of the church? You don't believe it? I'll show you right in your own Bible!

After the Jews were scattered and Gentile leaders began to take over the congregations, Yeshua had said that His disciples were not to be like the Gentiles, who lord over the flock: "Ye know that they which are accounted to rule over *the Gentiles exercise lordship over them*; and their *great ones exercise authority upon them*. But so shall it not be among you: but whosoever will be great among you, shall be your minister: And whosoever of you *will be the chiefest, shall be servant of all*" (Mark 10:42–44).

The problem was that most Gentile leaders had little to no foundation in the Torah to build on. One Greek pastor would not even allow the apostle John, or other Jews, in the church. He even kicked out any Gentile who would allow Jews in. Most people read right over the verses that tell us this. John wrote:

> I wrote to the church, but Diotrephes, who *loves to have the preeminence* among them, *receiveth us not*. Wherefore, if I come, I will remember his deeds, which he doeth, prating against us with malicious words; and not content with that, neither doth he himself *receive the brethren* [other Jews] and forbiddeth them that would, and casteth *them out of the church*. (3 John 9–10)

There it is! Even during John's time, the Gentiles were taking over the synagogues and kicking all the Jews out. For almost two thousand years now, there had been no Israel. In the absence of Israel, the church assumed that it must be the one to whom all the future promises refer. Then all of a sudden, through God's promises to the real Israel, the Jews became a nation again! What is the church to do? There's not room for both of us. That doesn't fit our theology.

The antagonism of the early Christians toward the Jews was reflected in the writings of the early "Church Fathers." Here are some examples:

Justin Martyr (c. AD 160), in speaking to a Jew, said: "The Scriptures are not yours, but ours."

Irenaeus, Bishop of Lyon (c. AD 177), declared: "Jews are disinherited from the grace of God."

Tertullian (AD 160–230), in his treatise Against the Jews, announced that God had rejected the Jews in favor of the Christians.

In the early fourth century, Eusebius wrote that the promises of the Hebrew Scriptures were for Christians and not the Jews; the curses were for the Jews. He argued that the church was the continuation of the Old Testament and thus superseded Judaism. The young church declared itself to be the true Israel, or "Israel according to the Spirit," heir to the divine promises. They found it essential to discredit the "Israel according to the flesh" to prove that God had cast away His people and transferred His love to the Christians.

In AD 306, Constantine became the first Christian Roman emperor. In AD 321, he made Christianity the official religion of the Empire, to the exclusion of all other religions. This signaled the end of the persecution of Christians, but the beginning of discrimination and persecution of the Jewish people. Let's take a look at how far off and how ignorant of the Scriptures Constantine really was.

In the book of Numbers, there were some men who were defiled by a dead body and therefore could not keep the Passover at the appointed time, so they asked Moses for a solution. He said:

Stand still, and I will hear what the LORD will command concerning you. And the LORD spake unto Moses, saying, Speak unto the children of Israel, saying, If any man of you or of your posterity shall be unclean by reason of a dead body, or be in a journey afar off, yet he shall keep the passover unto the LORD. The *fourteenth day of the second month* at even they shall keep it, and eat it with unleavened bread and bitter herbs. They shall leave none of it unto the morning, nor break any bone of it: according to all the ordinances of the passover they shall keep it. (Num. 9:8–12)

At the Lord's direction, these conscientious men were told they could keep the Passover in the second month. Several hundred years later this was still true:

And Hezekiah sent to all Israel and Judah, and wrote letters also to Ephraim and Manasseh, that they should come to the house of the LORD at Jerusalem, to keep the Passover unto the LORD God of Israel. For the king had taken counsel, and his princes, and all the congregation in Jerusalem, to keep the Passover in the second month. For they could not keep it at that time, because the priests had not sanctified themselves sufficiently, neither had the people gathered themselves together to Jerusalem. (2 Chr. 30:1–3)

Now before we go on, let me ask you: Are we to do what God says, or instead go by what is convenient for us? Should we go by what the majority says, or what God says? Do we do what seems reasonable to us, or to God? Are we to think of ourselves higher than others, or act in humility? Can we improve on what God does, or are any of us qualified to be His editor? Let's see what was determined at the Council of Nicea in AD 325. From the letter of the Emperor (Constantine) to all those not present at the council:

> When the question relative to the sacred festival of *Easter* arose, it was *universally* thought that *it would be convenient* that all should keep the feast on one day; it was declared to be particularly unworthy for this, the holiest of festivals, to follow the customs (the calculation) of the Jews who had soiled their hands with the most fearful of crimes, and whose minds were blinded. In *rejecting their custom* we may transmit to our descendants *the legitimate mode of celebrating Easter; We ought not therefore to have anything in common with the Jew, for the Saviour has shown us another way;* our worship following a *more legitimate* and *more convenient* course (the order of the days of the week: And consequently in unanimously adopting this mode, we desire, dearest brethren *to separate ourselves from the detestable company of the Jew.* For it is *truly shameful for us to hear them boast* that *without their direction we could not keep this feast.* How can they be in the right, they who, after the death of the Saviour, have no longer been led by reason but by wild violence, as their delusion may urge them? They do not possess the truth in this Easter question, *for in their blindness and repugnance to all improvements they frequently celebrate two Passovers in the same year.* We could not imitate those who are openly in error.
>
> How, then, could we follow these Jews who are most certainly blinded by error? For to celebrate a Passover twice in one year, is totally inadmissible. But even if this were not so it would still be your duty not to tarnish your soul by communication with such wicked people (the Jews). You should consider not only that the number of

churches in these provinces make a majority, but also that it is right to demand what our reason approves, and that we should have nothing in common with the Jews. (Found in Eusebius, Vita Const., Lib III 18–20)

Do you feel the love? Right here is when the church went grievously wrong, and they got us off the biblical calendar by doing what their human reason approved and by following what the majority ruled.

In the fourth century, the "church" told the Jewish people they could no longer determine the new moon or the biblical calendar, on pain of death. So Hillel II (AD 320–385), the *nasi*, or president, of the Great Sanhedrin determined that they would go back to the default position of the sun and moon to determine the feasts, as the Sanhedrin was threatened with extinction if they continued to sight the new moon. He established a fixed calendar based on the mathematical and astronomical calculations God had originally ordained. This calendar, still in use, standardized the length of months and the addition of months over the course of the nineteen-year cycle so that the lunar calendar consistently realigns with the solar years. Just as we add a leap day every four years, an entire month known as Adar II is added in the third, sixth, eighth, eleventh, fourteenth, seventeenth, and nineteenth years of the cycle. This is what keeps Passover in the spring as God required. We need to realize this is still the calendar God uses!

One day, Yeshua asked the crowd around Him, "Why call ye me, Lord, Lord, and do not the things which I say?" (Luke 6:46). One of those things He said, during His last

Passover meal, was, "This is my body which is given for you: this do in remembrance of me" (Luke 22:19).

The apostle Paul follows up with this comment in his first letter to the Corinthians: "For as often as ye eat this bread, and drink this cup, ye do shew the Lord's death till he come" (1 Cor. 11:26). We are to remember the Lord's death, and He died on Passover, which is Nisan 14 every year. If we reject the biblical calendar, how can we do what Yeshua asked? Most denominations never even hold a memorial Passover to remember the Lord's death as He commanded. Sure, we commemorate the resurrection at Easter, but why not celebrate the resurrection when it actually occurred, on the Feast of Firstfruits, when He became the firstfruits of the resurrection? Because we reject the biblical calendar, look what happens in 2016. Easter Sunday falls on March 27, so Christians will be celebrating the resurrection a month *before* Passover, the date that Christ died, which won't come until a month later, on April 21. Go figure! Christians won't be able to connect the signs coming from the heavens when they fall on Passover if they don't *make* the connections.

At El Shaddai we adhere to the biblical Jewish calendar because no individual has the authority to determine the calendar based on his own personal sighting of the moon, or the beginning of the New Year based on his own personal barley crop. You can't have hundreds of different people—especially those who have no authority or are not even Jewish—determining feast days. Even if I put on a police uniform and carry the laws of my state around, I cannot go around arresting people when I don't like how they drive, because I have no authority. Well, no one else has the authority to change the Jewish calendar. Just because someone carries a Torah scroll, wears a prayer shawl, and dons a *kippah* (skullcap), it does not give him the authority to determine the calendar.

Many of you who are new to all of this, please don't get caught up with all the Internet groups claiming they have the authority to decide when to celebrate the feasts. I've seen this for years. Someone learns how important it is to be on the biblical calendar, and the first thing he or she does is search the Internet and then gets caught up with a cult trying to manipulate and control the gullible. Stick with the original, and you won't go wrong. All of the biblically historic events that have happened over the centuries have occurred on the significant dates that fall on this calendar. In Genesis 1:14, God declared that the astronomical bodies, which cannot be controlled or manipulated by man, were the authority in declaring when the *moedim*, or festivals, were to be held. Think of the sun and the moon as the default position when there is no human authority to determine them. God later gave authority to Israel, while there was a legitimate Jewish court to do so, in determining when the feasts would take place.

Let's continue to examine some of the other early "church" fathers as we revisit the topic of anti-Semitism. Saint Jerome (AD 347–407) described the Jews as "serpents, wearing the image of Judas, their psalms and prayers are the braying of donkeys."

At the end of the fourth century, the Bishop of Antioch and great orator John Chrysostom wrote a series of eight sermons against the Jews. In his sermon titled "Against the

Jews" he wrote: "The synagogue is not only a brothel and a theater; it is also a den of robbers and a lodging for wild beasts. . . . No Jew adores God."

In the fifth century, the burning question was: If the Jews and Judaism were cursed by God, then how can you explain their continued existence? Augustine confronted this problem in his "Sermon against the Jews." He maintained that even though the Jews deserved the most severe punishment for having "killed our Jesus," they have been kept alive by Divine Providence to serve, together with their Scriptures, as witnesses to the truth of Christianity.

Remember what happened in 1492? Columbus sailed the ocean blue. Well, that's not all. Some say he was actually Jewish, as were the people who accompanied him. It is believed that King Ferdinand and Queen Isabella had signed an order, called the Alhambra Decree, that declared that all Jews had to leave Spain that year. The Inquisition was in full force, and any Jews who would not convert to Catholicism were put together in their synagogue, and they would burn every man, woman, and child within while they marched around, singing, "Christ, we adore thee." It was during this time that the Reformation was taking place and Martin Luther rejected Catholicism. He turned to the Jews, hoping they would accept his theology, and when they didn't, he wrote an exhaustive essay about his hatred for them, called *On the Jews and Their Lies* (1543). Here is an excerpt highlighting his vitriol:

> What shall we Christians do with this rejected and condemned people, the Jews? Since they live among us, we

dare not tolerate their conduct, now that we are aware of their lying and reviling and blaspheming. If we do, we become sharers in their lies, cursing and blasphemy. Thus we cannot extinguish the unquenchable fire of divine wrath, of which the prophets speak, nor can we convert the Jews.

With prayer and the fear of God we must practice a sharp mercy to see whether we might save at least a few from the glowing flames. We dare not avenge ourselves. Vengeance a thousand times worse than we could wish them already has them by the throat. I shall give you my sincere advice:

First to set fire to their synagogues or schools and to bury and cover with dirt whatever will not burn, so that no man will ever again see a stone or cinder of them. This is to be done in honor of our Lord and of Christendom, so that God might see that we are Christians, and do not condone or knowingly tolerate such public lying, cursing, and blaspheming of his Son and of his Christians. For whatever we tolerated in the past unknowingly—and I myself was unaware of it—will be pardoned by God. . . .

Second, I advise that their houses also be razed and destroyed. For they pursue in them the same aims as in their synagogues. Instead they might be lodged under a roof or in a barn, like the gypsies. This will bring home to them that they are not masters in our country, as they boast, but that they are living in exile and in captivity, as they incessantly wail and lament about us before God.

Third, I advise that all their prayer books and Talmudic writings, in which such idolatry, lies, cursing and blasphemy are taught, be taken from them.

Fourth, I advise that their rabbis be forbidden to teach henceforth on pain of loss of life and limb. For they have justly forfeited the right to such an office by holding the poor Jews captive with the saying of Moses. They wantonly employ the poor people's obedience contrary to the law of the Lord and infuse them with this poison, cursing, and blasphemy. . . .

Fifth, I advise that safe-conduct on the highways be abolished completely for the Jews. For they have no business in the countryside, since they are not lords, officials, tradesmen, or the like. Let they stay at home. . . .

Sixth, I advise that usury be prohibited to them, and that all cash and treasure of silver and gold be taken from them and put aside for safekeeping. . . .

Seventh, I commend putting a flail, an ax, a hoe, a spade, a distaff, or a spindle into the hands of young, strong Jews and Jewesses and letting them earn their bread in the sweat of their brow, as was imposed on the children of Adam. For it is not fitting that they should let us accursed Goyim toil in the sweat of our faces while they, the holy people, idle away their time behind the stove, feasting and farting, and on top of all, boasting blasphemously of their lordship over the Christians by means of our sweat. . . .

Burn down their synagogues, forbid all that I enumerated earlier, force them to work, and deal harshly with them, as Moses did in the wilderness, slaying three thousand lest the whole people perish. They surely do not know what they are doing; moreover, as people possessed, they do not wish to know it, hear it, or learn it. There it would be wrong to be merciful and confirm them in their conduct. If this does not help we must drive them out like mad dogs, so that we do not become partakers of their abominable blasphemy and all their other vices and thus merit God's wrath and be damned with them. I have done my duty. Now let everyone see to his. I am exonerated."[1]

The Bible declares that there is nothing new under the sun. Anti-semitism was happening back then, and it is happening today. We are only building upon the sins of the fathers. There is a saying that *the Church* started it all with forced conversions, declaring: "Jews cannot live among us as Jews!"

Then *the nations* of the world followed up on what the church said and declared, "The Jews cannot live among us!"

Then *Hitler* simply built on the foundation the Church had already laid and simply stated, "Jews cannot live."

Even Saint Thomas Aquinas declared that the Jews should be held in perpetual servitude and that their possessions belonged to the State.

Well, do you feel the love? The Bible warns Christians about not being pretentious and thinking they are better than the branches:

> Boast not against the branches. But if thou boast, thou bearest not the root, but the root thee. Thou wilt say then, The branches were broken off, that I might be graffed in. Well; because of unbelief they were broken off, and thou standest by faith. Be not highminded, but

---

1   Martin Luther, *On the Jews and Their Lies*, Martin H. Bertram, trans., in *Luther's Works*, vol. 47 (Minneapolis: Augsburg Fortress, 1971), http://www.humanitas-international.org/showcase/chronography/documents/luther-jews.htm.

fear: For if God spared not the natural branches, take heed lest he also spare not thee. (Rom. 11:18–21)

And people ask me, "How come the Jews don't get it?" Here is one reason why:

For as ye in times past have not believed God, yet have now obtained mercy through their unbelief: Even so have these also now not believed, that through your mercy they also may obtain mercy. For God hath concluded them all in unbelief, that he might have mercy upon all. (Rom. 11:30–32)

Did you catch that? Because of the unbelief of the Jews, Gentiles were granted mercy. Then it goes on to say when the Gentiles who have received mercy show mercy to the Jewish people, they will believe. A big reason why Jewish people do not believe in the Messiah is Christians have rarely shown them mercy! We generally have only shown judgment, kicking them out from nation to nation and killing them all in the honor of the Lord.

I asked a rabbi one time why Jewish leaders don't mind if Jews become Buddhists but they are upset if they become Christians. His answer surprised me. He said, "Because the Buddhists don't kill us!"

Putting all of this in perspective, let's look at the attitude Moses had when God Himself was ready to disinherit the Jewish people after the sin of the spies, when they all wanted to stone Joshua and Caleb:

But all the congregation bade stone them with stones. And the glory of the LORD appeared in the tabernacle of the congregation before all the children of Israel. And the LORD said unto Moses, How long will this people provoke me? and how long will it be ere they believe me, *for all the signs which I have showed among them*? I will smite them with the pestilence, and *disinherit them*, and *will make of you a greater* nation and mightier than they. (Num. 14:10–12)

In other words, "Moses, you will be *great!*"

Now, Moses could have said, "Wahoo! Go get 'em, God!" But how did He react instead?

Then the Egyptians will hear it, for by Your might You brought these people up from among them, and they will tell it to the inhabitants of this land. They have heard that You, LORD, are among these people; that You, LORD, are seen face to face and Your cloud stands above them, and You go before them in a pillar of cloud by day and in a pillar of fire by night. "Now if You kill these people as one man, then the nations which have heard of Your fame will speak, saying, *Because the LORD was not able to bring this people to the land which He swore to give them, therefore He killed them in the wilderness.*' (Num. 14:13–16)

Moses was more concerned about God's reputation than his own. Look at what he goes on to say:

And now, I pray, let the power of my Lord be great, just as You have spoken, saying, The Lord is longsuffering and abundant in mercy, forgiving iniquity and transgression; but He by no means clears the guilty, visiting the iniquity of the fathers on the children to the third and fourth generation.

Pardon the iniquity of this people, I pray, according to the greatness of Your mercy, just as You have forgiven this people, from Egypt even until now.

Then the Lord said: I have pardoned, according to your word; but truly, as I live, all the earth shall be filled with the glory of the Lord. (Num. 14:17–21)

The "church" needs to take its cues from Moses and be more concerned with God's reputation in the fulfilling of His promises to the Jewish people than in inflating their own egos. The fathers of our faith are in reality Abraham, Isaac, and Jacob.

Here is just one more reason why we need to be on God's calendar and be connected to the Torah as well. Historical events line up with the Torah readings for the week. I believe following the biblical calendar is like an alignment you may get at a chiropractor. Everything falls into place. There was an incredible alignment that took place in 2012. On Saturday, March 24, 2012, the Torah reading was *Vayikra*, or the beginning of the book of Leviticus. Vayikra means "and he called" and refers to the first words of the first verse in Leviticus. Now look at all these coincidences. It just "so happened" that March 24 was a Shabbat, the Torah portion was Leviticus 1:1–5:26, and it was the first of Nisan. What happened on the first of Nisan?

And the Lord spake unto Moses, saying, On the first day of the first month shalt thou set up the tabernacle of the tent of the congregation. (Ex. 40:1–2)

Leviticus 1 is a continuation of Exodus 40, happening on the same day that Moses set up the tabernacle. So March 24, 2012, was a Sabbath; it was also Nisan 1—the very day Moses actually assembled the tabernacle—and the Torah reading for that day was of Moses assembling the tabernacle! So here we were, reading the exact instructions given to Moses by God on *the very day*, from the *very Torah portion* in which the event actually occurred! How often does this happen? The next time this will take place will be March 21, 2015. That day will again be a Sabbath, the first of Nisan, the very day Moses set up the tabernacle. And again the reading will be about the tabernacle being assembled, and additionally, it will be kicked off with the total solar eclipse—followed two weeks later by the total lunar eclipse on Passover. This is too incredible!

You don't know what you don't know. This is why I ask the body of Messiah to try being on God's calendar for one year and experience the most incredible walk you will ever have. In Amos, it says, "Can two walk together unless they be agreed?" (3:3). If you come in agreement with the calendar God uses, you will become exceedingly close to the Lord in your walk.

Several years ago, at least fifty churches read from the Koran in their Sunday services to show their solidarity with Islam. I thought it was the stupidest thing I'd ever heard of. They should have all read from the Torah to show their solidarity with Israel; after all, we at least share the same book. In response to the Koran reading, I organized a Torah reading in churches around the country. I thought, *What is the greatest verse both Jews and Christians have in common?*

Of course it would have to be the Shema, the greatest commandment: "Thou shalt love the LORD thy God with all thine heart, and with all thy soul, and with all thy might" (Deut. 6:5). I didn't just want to have it read on any random Sunday, but I wanted it to be read the very same weekend all the Jews around the world were reading it. So in the summer of 2011, the very same weekend the Jews were reading the greatest commandment in their synagogues, churches all over the world joined in reading the greatest commandment: to love the Lord our God! We received videos from all over of people trying to read the Shema in Hebrew. This word means both "to hear" and "to obey."

May we all hear and obey these words.

6
THE SCIENCE OF THE SIGNS

The Jewish calendar is more complicated than our Gregorian calendar, but God has a reason for everything He does. There are three heavenly events on which the Jewish calendar is based: the rotation of the earth makes a day, the rotation of the moon around the earth makes a month, and the rotation of the earth around the sun makes a year. (The Gregorian calendar follows the first and third events.) It takes about 29½ days for the moon to revolve around the earth and 365¼ days for the earth to revolve around the sun. The Jewish calendar handles the fractions by using either 29- or 30-day months and either 12- or 13-month years.

Scientifically, you can only have a solar eclipse at a new moon or the first day of a biblical month, and you can only have a total lunar eclipse at a full moon on the fifteenth day of a biblical month. This is why God scheduled some of His divine appointments or feast days at those times. Rosh Hashanah is the first day of the seventh month. And both Passover (the Feast of Unleavened Bread) and the Feast of Tabernacles are on the fifteenth of the biblical month. Solar and lunar eclipses are common occurrences for the most part and have no great prophetic significance. However, when they fall on feast days, we should pay close attention, because God is trying to tell us something.

According to NASA, there are three types of lunar eclipses:

1. Penumbral: the moon traverses Earth's penumbral shadow (it misses Earth's umbral shadow)

2. Partial: the moon traverses Earth's penumbral and umbral shadows (it does not pass completely into Earth's umbra)

3. Total: the moon traverses Earth's penumbral and umbral shadows (it passes completely into Earth's umbra)[1]

During the five-millennium period from 2000 BC to AD 3000, we will experience 12,064 of one of the three types of lunar eclipses, averaging about 2.4 a year. Over a period of five thousand years, from 1999 BC to AD 3000, there will be a total of 3,479 total lunar eclipses. As you may recall from the introduction, four consecutive *total* lunar eclipses in a row, without any partial or penumbral eclipses in between, are known as a tetrad.

It is not uncommon for eclipses to fall on feast days since God designed those holidays to fall on days when lunar

---

1   "Eclipse Predictions by Fred Espenak (NASA's GSFC)," http://eclipse.gsfc.nasa. gov/LEcat5/LEcatalog.html.

eclipses would take place. But four total lunar eclipses in a row are not as common as one would believe. Among the 3,479 eclipses over five thousand years, there will only be 142 tetrads. There were 62 tetrads over the last two thousand years. Of these, only eight fell on feast days, with the ninth coming in 2014–2015.

"So, what's the big deal?" you might ask. Let's look at the significance of the number 9 in Scripture. In his book *Number in Scripture* (Grand Rapids: Kregel, 1967, 1980), author E. W. Bullinger explained:

> The number *nine* . . . is the *last* of the [single] digits, and thus marks the *end*; and is significant of the *conclusion* of a matter.
>
> It is akin to the number *six*, six being the sum of its factors (3 x 3 = 9, and 3 + 3 = 6), and is thus significant of the *end of man*, and the summation of all man's works. *Nine* is, therefore,
>
> THE NUMBER OF FINALITY OR JUDGMENT . . .
>
> It marks the completeness, the end and issue of all things as to man—the judgment of man and all his works.
>
> It is a *factor* of 666, which is 9 times 74. . . .
>
> The sum of the 22 letters of the Hebrew alphabet is 4995 (5 x 999). It is stamped, therefore, with the numbers of *grace* and *finality*. (p. 235)

Before I get too far ahead of myself, let's look at some of the extremely important eclipses that occurred on biblical holidays in the first century. While there were not four total lunar eclipses in a row, some of the eclipses did happen during very significant feast days in very auspicious years. We know the Temple was destroyed in AD 70. Around eight months before that event, on our October 18 in AD 69, there was a partial lunar eclipse on the Feast of Sukkot. A total solar eclipse followed this on Nisan 1, or March 30, in AD 70, the beginning of the religious year. Two weeks later, there was a penumbral lunar eclipse on Passover, which fell on April 4. An annular solar eclipse followed this on Rosh Hashanah, our September 23, then another penumbral lunar eclipse on Sukkot, October 8. This is totally verifiable by NASA. But that's not all! Another partial lunar eclipse appeared on Purim the following year, on our March 4 in AD 71. A hybrid solar eclipse was seen on Nisan 1, or March 20, followed by another hybrid solar eclipse on Rosh Hashanah, on our September 12! Talk about signs of astronomical proportions happening on the feast days around the destruction of the Temple!

The following chart lays out the time frame around the destruction of the Temple:

GREGORIAN DATE	HEAVENLY EVENT	BIBLICAL DATE
OCTOBER 18, AD 69	PARTIAL LUNAR ECLIPSE	SUKKOT
MARCH 30, AD 70	TOTAL SOLAR ECLIPSE	NISAN 1
APRIL 14, AD 70	PENUMBRAL LUNAR ECLIPSE	PASSOVER
TEMPLE DESTROYED 9TH OF AV		
SEPTEMBER 21, AD 70	ANNUAL SOLAR ECLIPSE	ROSH HASHANAH
OCTOBER 8, AD 70	PENUMBRAL LUNAR ECLIPSE	SUKKOT
MARCH 4, AD 71	PARTIAL LUNAR ECLIPSE	PURIM
MARCH 20, AD 71	HYBRID SOLAR ECLIPSE	NISAN 1
SEPTEMBER 12, AD 71	HYBRID SOLAR ECLIPSE	ROSH HASHANAH

Now here is another mindblower. I don't know for sure if anyone can pinpoint the exact year when Yeshua died, but most would put it between AD 30 and 33. Astonishingly, in AD 32, there was a solar eclipse on Nisan 1, followed by a total lunar eclipse on Passover. Then there was another solar eclipse on Rosh Hashanah, followed by a total lunar eclipse on Sukkot. In AD 33, a total solar eclipse again appeared on Nisan 1, followed by a partial lunar eclipse on Passover, an annular solar eclipse on Rosh Hashanah, and another partial lunar eclipse on Sukkot! The odds of the eclipses tied to the feast days in those years are statistically off the charts!

GREGORIAN YEAR	HEAVENLY EVENT	JEWISH FEAST
AD 32	SOLAR ECLIPSE	NISAN 1
AD 32	TOTAL LUNAR ECLIPSE	PASSOVER
AD 32	SOLAR ECLIPSE	ROSH HASHANAH
AD 32	TOTAL LUNAR ECLIPSE	SUKKOT
AD 33	TOTAL SOLAR ECLIPSE	NISAN 1
AD 33	PARTIAL LUNAR ECLIPSE	PASSOVER
AD 33	ANNULAR SOLAR ECLIPSE	ROSH HASHANAH
AD 33	PARTIAL LUNAR ECLIPSE	SUKKOT

If we are not on the biblical calendar, we lose all the significance of the totally incredible signs God is revealing to us.

Here is a quick synopsis of the sixty-two tetrads that have occurred over the last two thousand years and will occur through AD 2100:

There were no tetrads in the first century, but between AD 100 and 200 there were three, in the years 162–63,

180–81, and 198–99. Of these three, only the first fell on Passover and Sukkot, respectively.

In the three-hundred-year stretch between AD 200 and 500, there was a total of thirteen tetrads, but none of them fell on feast days. There were no tetrads during the next two hundred years.

From AD 700 to 800, there were just three tetrads, with one occurring on the Feast of Passover and Sukkot, in AD 795–96. The next century, though, showed quite a flurry of tetrads, with a total of eight. Only twice, though, did they occur on feast days: in 842–43 and 860–61.

In 843, the Treaty of Verdun was signed to end the Carolinigian civil war and divide the Carolingian Empire into three kingdoms: West Francia, Middle Francia, and East Francia. The Carolingians were tolerant to their Jewish subjects, but the division of the empire adversely affected all the Jews in the realm.

From 900 to 1000, there were six tetrads, but none occurred on the feast days. There were no tetrads for the next three hundred years. Then, from 1300 to 1400, there were six tetrads, but again, none fell on the feast days.

Between 1400 and 1500 there were four tetrads, two of which fell on the feast days: 1428–29 and 1493–94. Interestingly, it was in 1428 that an assembly of Jews in Italy met in Florence to gather funds to give to Pope Martin V in return for his protection. And in 1492, when Columbus sailed the ocean, King Ferdinand and Queen Isabella signed an edict to expel all the Jews from Spain. This was a very significant event in Jewish history. As mentioned previously, many believe that Columbus was Jewish, as well as a number of his passengers.

From 1500 to 1600, there were six tetrads, without any appearing on the feast days. Then there were no tetrads for three hundred years. That brings us to modern history. Between 1900 and 2000 there were five tetrads, but only two occurred on feast days—1949–50 and 1967–68. These were epic years for the Jewish people, with major prophetic implications. In 1948, Israel became a nation, and then in 1967, the Israelites recaptured Jerusalem. Not only do we have four blood moons in a row, with all four of them falling on feast days, but they also happened at a time when historic prophecies were fulfilled!

In this century, eight tetrads will occur, but the only time they will fall on the feast days is in 2014–15.

The following chart offers a recap of the tetrads since the first century:

CENTURY	NUMBER OF TETRADS	NUMBER OF TIMES ON FEAST DAYS	NUMBER OF TIMES ON PASSOVER AND SUKKOT
1ST	0		
2ND	3	1	162–63
3RD	6		
4TH	4		
5TH	3		
6TH	0		
7TH	0		
8TH	3	1	795–96
9TH	8	2	842–43 AND 860–61
10TH	6		
11TH	0		
12TH	0		
13TH	0		
14TH	6		
15TH	4	2	1428–29 AND 1493–94
16TH	6		
17TH	0		
18TH	0		
19TH	0		
20TH	5	2	1949–50 AND 1967–68
21ST	8	1	2014–15

Here is a snapshot of some of the columns that I saw when I looked at the NASA website in 2008 for the occurrences of lunar eclipses happening over the next ten years:

CALENDAR DATE	ECLIPSE TYPE	SAROS CYCLE	GEOGRAPHIC REGION
2014 APRIL 15	TOTAL	122	AUSTRALIA, PACIFIC, AMERICAS
2014 OCT 8	TOTAL	127	ASIA, AUSTRALIA, PACIFIC, AMERICAS
2015 APRIL 4	TOTAL	132	ASIA, AUSTRALIA, PACIFIC, AMERICAS
2015 SEPT 28	TOTAL	137	PACIFIC, AMERICAS, EUROPE, W. ASIA

The saros **cycle** is a period of 223 synodic months or a period of 18 years, 11 days, and 8 hours. One synodic month is the time from one new moon to the next new moon. The saros cycle can be used to predict eclipses of the sun and moon. A saros **series** is made up of three saros cycles. In the following saros cycle chart you will see nine saros cycles, beginning in 1901 on the bottom right and ending in 2045 in the upper left. As you will see, the eclipses visibility moves to the west with each new cycle. When the saros series is complete (after three cycles or about 54 years and 34 days) the eclipses return to approximately the same geographic region.

Figure 1 — Eclipses from Saros 136: 1901 to 2045

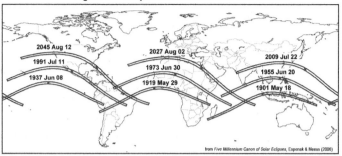

from *Five Millennium Canon of Solar Eclipses*, Espenak & Meeus (2006)

Much like a giant clock, the saros cycle keeps coming back to it's original location. Look at the following chart I made of the saros cycle 137 that includes the total super moon eclipse happening on Sukkot in 2015. Also notice the eighteen-year intervals as mentioned and when they fall on the biblical calendar.

SAROS 137	HEBREW MONTH	# MONTH
JULY 2 1871	TAMMUZ	4TH
JULY 12 1889	TAMMUZ	4TH
JULY 25 1906	AV	5TH
AUG 4 1925	AV	5TH
AUG 15 1943	AV	5TH
SEPT 6 1979	ELUL	6TH
SEPT 16 1997	ELUL	6TH
SEPT 28 2015	TISHRI	7TH
OCT 8 2033	TISHRI	7TH

Notice the repeat of the Hebrew months and what month they are on the calendar. You see it looks like a clock ticking by with every generation of around fifty years being a single month. Think of a clock where the months of the year represent each five-minute interval. Using the biblical calendar or God's time clock, see that we have twelve Hebrew months and twelve divisions on a clock. The month of Tishri was the first month of Creation (Adam was created on the first of Tishri) so it is only appropriate we begin there. The months of Av and Elul are the last two months of the civil calendar.

Everyone asks how close we are to midnight as far as the coming of the LORD. Let's put it on our Hebrew time clock and see how close we are to Tishri where all the fall feasts that speak of the LORD's return occur. The Hebrew calendar months are measured from new moon to new moon, which is about 29.53 days or one synodic month. As I mentioned above, 223 synodic months is a saros cycle or 18 years and 11 days. Three saros cycles, or 54 years and a few days over 1 month is a saros series. So let's also look at our time clock with the sun in the center. It takes twelve months, or one solar year, for the earth to go around the sun. Now, think of the clock where each saros series (three saros cycles, roughly 54 years) represents each five-minute interval.

Now that you see how the cycles of the moon are like a clock ticking down, let's add the time periods for the saros series. Remember that Creation happened in the month of Tishri. That is why it is the first month on our clock. If you begin counting the generations from the time of creation,

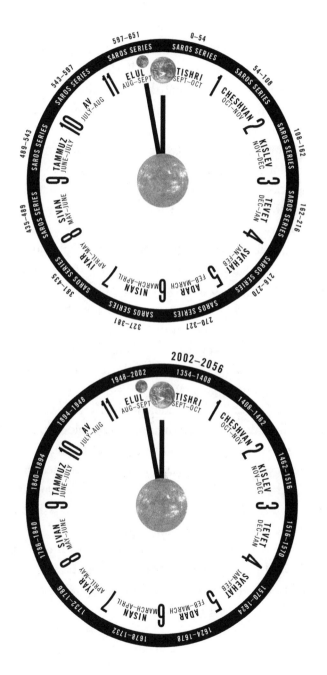

you end up with the generation from 1354 to 1408 falling in the saros series in the month of Tishri (or from midnight to one o'clock). Notice that the generational time period, from 1894 to 1948, falls in the month of Av. As you recall, the month of Av is the month of the destruction of the Temple being destroyed twice even on the same day. Av speaks of judgment. The generation from 1894 to 1948 was a generation of judgment. During that time, we had the two most destructive wars the world had ever seen: World War I and World War II. The next month is the month of Elul. Elul is known as the month of return. Often after judgment we return back to God. What happened during the time period from 1948 to the year 2002? Israel returned back to her land and Jerusalem returned into Jewish hands. This leads us to the next generation. The generation from 2002 to 2056 will be the generation where the month of Tishri will be fulfilled! The fall feasts and the return of the Messiah will happen in this generation!

From Joel 2:31, we understand that the sun shall be turned into darkness and the moon into blood before the great and the terrible day of the LORD come. This is an exciting correlation between the signs in the heavens that God said He would use and His calendar that He created for us to use as His decoder! This way we know it is not a random occurrence but a godly appointment!

While contemplating these lunar eclipses I realized that the Bible also said there would be a sign in the sun! So back I raced to the NASA website specifically looking at the year 2015. Here is what I found:

CALENDAR DATE	ECLIPSE TYPE	GEOGRAPHIC REGION
2015 MARCH 20	TOTAL	ICELAND, EUROPE, N. AFRICA, N. ASIA
2015 SEPT 13	PARTIAL	S. AFRICA, S. INDIAN, ANTACTICA

As you can see, in 2015 we have a total solar eclipse on March 20 followed by a partial solar eclipse on September 13. But I hope that you are asking yourself right now the same question that I did, "But when do they fall on the Biblical calendar?"

The total solar eclipse—March 20, 2015—is on Nisan 1; the very beginning of the religious year and the very day the fire fell from heaven and lit the altar at the dedication of Moses' tabernacle! Following that, there will be a partial solar eclipse on September 13, 2015, which is on Rosh Hashanah. After that, just two weeks later, there will be a total lunar eclipse on Sukkot! This just rocks!

In summary, we have had only eight tetrads in the last two thousand years that fell on the feast days. Major prophetic events have occurred on or around the last three tetrads over the past five hundred years. The ninth tetrad starts on Passover in 2014. Have you ever heard of a supermoon? The distance of the moon from the Earth varies throughout the month and year. Since the moon orbits the earth in an elliptical pattern, sometimes it is closer to the earth than others. When it is closest to the earth at the full moon stage, it is referred to as super full moon or supermoon.

The odds of a full moon are about 1 in 29. The odds of

a lunar eclipse are about 1 in 110. The odds of a supermoon occurrence are about 1 in 6,570. The odds of a supermoon during a lunar eclipse are, well, astronomical. Now think about this. What are the odds of having this super blood moon also falling on the Feast of Tabernacles! This is beyond coincidence. Now think about having this super blood moon, the largest of the year, falling on the Feast of Tabernacles, and being seen in Jerusalem while everyone is outside in their sukkahs looking up to the heavens. This is what is going to happen on the Feast of Tabernacles in 2015. Can you imagine what it will be like for the Jewish people in Israel sitting in their sukkahs on the first night of the Feast of Tabernacles and there is this super blood moon overhead? Don't you think God is trying to speak to us? This is equivalent to a prophetic grand slam homerun. The heavens are shouting, "Hello! Is anybody paying attention?"

Coincidence? Maybe. But before you make that your "final answer," read on.

7
FOR THE NAYSAYERS

Since my discovery in March 2008 of the correlation between eclipses past and future and when they fall on the biblical calendar, there have been many naysayers. One of the first objections I heard was that "this is only Mark Biltz's theory." But the facts don't lie. That eclipses actually occur is a fact. That they fall on *feast days* according to the biblical calendar is also a fact. The biblical calendar is not a theory. It is a fact that when eclipses have fallen on past feast days, major historical events have happened. I do not control eclipses, and I do not have authority over the biblical calendar. The only theory I hold is what significance these events may have, which I will discuss later.

Another objection I've heard is that I am a false prophet. But *I* am not prophesying the coming eclipses. NASA has scientifically determined when they will occur. Neither am I am prophesying that they will fall on biblical holidays. It is not I who determines when they fall. I am not a prophet, nor do I claim to be one. I am just letting the world know a pattern exists between when eclipses have fallen on past feast days and major events that have occurred at the same time. As far as what will happen during the next tetrad, that is up to the reader to contemplate and pray about. Now, of course it is fun to speculate on what it all may mean, but that is no more prophesying than trying to guess who will win a football game. (Go, Seahawks!)

Other grumblers protest that not all of the four eclipses in the upcoming tetrad will be seen in Jerusalem. So what? They weren't all seen in Israel when that tiny country became a Jewish nation in 1948, and they weren't all seen in Jerusalem when the Jews recaptured it in 1967! Still, everyone would agree that these were extremely significant prophetic events. And if you didn't see them, well sorry, you missed it. God will do what He wants to whether we like it or not, know it or not, see it or not, or even care. This is a very narrow view of prophecy anyway. God loves the whole world, not just the Jewish people. And that the eclipses will not *all* be visible in Jerusalem is a moot point, because with the advent of technology, everyone in Jerusalem—or for that matter, anyone with an Internet connection anywhere in the world—will be able to see every one of these eclipses. Even without technology, every part of the world will see at least one of them. God is announcing His signals to *all* tribes, tongues, and nations. Remarkably, the final blood moon on the Feast of Tabernacles in 2015 *will* be seen from Jerusalem. And it will be a supermoon! While it is not larger, it has the appearance of being around 14 percent larger.

Some readers say the eclipses are irrelevant because one time a significant event might come *after* the four blood moons, and another time it might occur *before* them. This is also totally missing the point. Think of it this way: America or the United Nations may think that *they* should get the credit (or blame, depending on how you look at it) for creating Israel in 1948, but the fact that these four blood moons occurred in 1949 and 1950 is, I believe, God's way of telling the world it was *His* doing and had nothing to do with the United Nations! They were mere puppets in the hand of God! In 1967, when the first of the four blood moons occurred a few months before the Six-Day War, God was telling the nation of Israel that His hands were going to be all over it. Sadly, these signals were totally missed by everyone anyway, as the connections were not made until I discovered them in 2008. At least this time we have a forewarning of what may come!

Another objection I encounter is from people who are reading what others are saying about the eclipses, and I have nothing to do with their statements. A lot of folks will read articles by writers who misquote me or assume I am saying things that I am not, and then they get all fired up and accuse me of saying things I never said. People really need to check their sources and contact me before spreading rumors.

"You're saying that a biblically significant event will happen on the very day the eclipses occur," other folks complain. No, I am not. As noted before, the four blood moons of 1949–50 occurred *after* Israel became a nation in 1948. The Six-Day War of 1967 did not happen on the day of one of the eclipses either. The eclipses coming in 2014 and 2015 are signs in themselves, as they occur on the feast days. If nothing noteworthy happens in 2014 or 2015, it just means these are signs of things to come.

Then there are the debunkers, and I now have to debunk

the debunkers. Some people object the idea that the eclipses occur around major events because they aren't tied to the seven seals in Revelation. The reason I never tried to tie the eclipses to the seals is because that wasn't my point, which they totally missed. I wasn't making predictions or connections to any seals or trumpets in the book of Revelation. My point is to demonstrate that God says He created the sun and the moon to send signals on His feast days. And guess what? There are some big signals coming that will start flashing like a billboard, and if people focus on the seals and not the feast days, they'll be left in the dark.

Still other people say I am setting dates for when Yeshua will return and will rapture all the saints. No, I am not. I have never set dates and never will. "No one knows the day or the hour," my accusers chide. Exactly! I have never said I knew the day or the hour. I have no idea when the rapture will happen. The only dates I am setting are when the eclipses will occur on the biblical calendar. Again, it will be exciting if the eclipses and the rapture *do* happen at the same time, and if you want to think so, more power to you, but one thing I realized a long time ago was that God is not going to consult me as to when He should either come back or raise the dead. I will point out, though, that God is the same yesterday, today, and forever. If He fulfilled the spring feasts to the day with His first coming, then it makes sense that He would fulfill all the fall feasts to the day with His second coming. Look at what Paul wrote to the Thessalonians: "But of the *times and the seasons, brethren*, ye have no need that I write unto you. For yourselves know perfectly that the day of the Lord so cometh as a thief in the night" (1 Thess. 5:1–2).

Hopefully by now you realize that when he mentions "times and seasons" he is speaking about the appointed times and the festivals of the Lord. Why does he say there is "no need" for him to write to the church about the feasts? Because they get it! He goes on to say: "But ye, brethren, are not in darkness, that that day should overtake you as a thief" (v. 4). Read that several times!

There are three fall feasts that must be fulfilled at Messiah's coming:

1. The Feast of Trumpets (Do you read anything about trumpets in the book of Revelation?)

2. The Feast of Yom Kippur (Israel's national day to be atoned for)

3. The Feast of Tabernacles (when God tabernacles among men for a thousand years)

I have no doubt that different biblical prophetic events will happen on these very days. So yes, I do know the *days* that events will happen, but I am still not setting dates, because I have no idea what year! All I know is that God is the same yesterday, today, and forever, and there is no shadow of turning with Him!

Many people speculate on where I am regarding the timing of the rapture. As I said in chapter 4, it doesn't matter to me. Why do I say that? Because I am not afraid. When a house is on fire, you have people running out and others running in. It depends on what you believe your calling is. I believe the time of Jacob's trouble will be the

"Super Bowl" of human history, and I don't want to miss it. For me, it's "Put me in the game, Coach!" I just want to finish the task God has given me to do. If I finish it beforehand, great; take me out. In the middle, that's fine too. If it's at the end, okay, Lord. Just let me finish the task You have given me to do. I really believe it will be like when Philip baptized the Ethiopian eunuch and then was transported to another city. We could be facing danger, and God will transport us to another city. Who wants to miss that?

I used to think how amazing it will be to sit down at the wedding supper of the Lamb with Abraham, Isaac, and Jacob and hear all their stories. Now I realize, as the Bible says, that even the angels desire to look into the things that are happening in this world as prophecy unfolds. They are waiting excitedly to talk to us and ask us what it was like to participate in the terminal generation, where all of prophecy culminated. I don't want to tell them, "I don't know, because I hid behind a rock!" I pray this book is a wake-up call to all the men and women of valor out there who know no fear and who are willing to rise up to the most glorious assignment of joining the heavenly army and fulfilling the task God has called them to do!

Having had two relatives die in the Holocaust, I will never stand idly by while the enemy attacks! Never again will the Jewish people go down as lambs to the slaughter on my watch. I'm in this to the glorious end. We are all going to die anyway, so let's go in glory! For believers, there is no need to be afraid of death. We just change clothes, so to speak. My only fear is not having completed the job God gave me to do.

Too many Christians waste so much time trying to determine when the rapture is going to take place that they get absolutely nothing done for the kingdom. There are no extra points for being right. And if you are wrong, it doesn't mean you won't be raised from the dead. I would rather be wrong and ready than right and unprepared. God does not care about my personal view of the rapture anyway. He only cares if I am doing what He told me to do.

8
THE CONCLUSION OF THE MATTER

"To every thing there is a season, and a time to every purpose under the heaven" (Eccl. 3:1). We now know how true this is. For God, it is all about the times and seasons for His every purpose. This is why Paul says that "concerning *the times and the seasons*, brethren, you have no need that I should write to you" (1 Thess. 5:1). As I said in the previous chapter, he is talking about the feasts of the Lord! In this chapter, I want to tell you a little more about the shemittah year and how important it is to God.

We find in Leviticus "Six years thou shalt sow thy field, and six years thou shalt prune thy vineyard, and gather in the fruit thereof; but in the seventh year shall be a sabbath of rest unto the land, a sabbath for the LORD: thou shalt neither sow thy field, nor prune thy vineyard" (Lev. 25:3–4). The seventh year, or shemittah, was also to be a time when the servants were set free: "If thou buy an Hebrew servant, six years he shall serve: and in the seventh he shall go out free for nothing" (Ex. 21:2). Because Israel did not obey this commandment, they had to spend seventy years exiled in Babylon. We see God's judgment pronounced in the book of Jeremiah:

Thus saith the LORD, the God of Israel; I made a covenant with your fathers in the day that I brought them forth out of the land of Egypt, out of the house of bondmen, saying, At the end of seven years let ye go every man his brother an Hebrew, which hath been sold unto thee; and when he hath served thee six years, thou shalt let him go free from thee: but your fathers hearkened not unto me, neither inclined their ear. And ye were now turned, and had done right in my sight, in proclaiming liberty every man to his neighbour; and ye had made a covenant before me in the house which is called by my name: But ye turned and polluted my name, and caused every man his servant, and every man his handmaid, whom ye had set at liberty at their pleasure, to return, and brought them into subjection, to be unto you for servants and for handmaids. Therefore thus saith the LORD; Ye have not hearkened unto me, in proclaiming liberty, every one to his brother, and every man to his neighbour: behold, I proclaim a liberty for you, saith the LORD, to the sword, to the pestilence, and to the famine; and I will make you to be removed into all the kingdoms of the earth. (Jer. 34:13–17)

God foretold this in Leviticus 26:33–35: "And I will scatter you among the heathen, and will draw out a sword after you: and your land shall be desolate, and your cities waste. Then shall the land enjoy her Sabbaths, as long as it lieth desolate, and ye be in your enemies' land; even then shall the land rest, and enjoy her Sabbaths. As long as it lieth desolate it shall rest; because it did not rest in your Sabbaths, when ye dwelt upon it."

Daniel understood this when he referred to Jeremiah: "In the first year of his reign I Daniel understood by books the number of the years, whereof the word of the LORD came to Jeremiah the prophet, that he would accomplish seventy years in the desolations of Jerusalem" (Dan. 9:2). This sabbath year, or shemittah, has become a year of judgment instead of a year of blessing for those who do not obey. There is an incredible connection here.

Many of you may remember the comet Shoemaker-Levy 9, which broke into pieces. This historic event took place from July 16 through July 22, 1994. Twenty-one fragments had catastrophic effects as they collided with Jupiter. It just so happens that weekend was also the weekend of the ninth of Av, and it was a shemittah year! Not only that, the Torah portion for that weekend was Deuteronomy 1–6, which in Hebrew is called *Devarim*, which means "These are the words." It is almost as if the Lord was saying, "Listen to Me: I am speaking to you about coming judgment." Seven times three is twenty-one, so I felt that God was saying that the next three shemittahs would be times of judgment. So what happened in the next shemittah year?

On September 17, 2001, or Elul 29, the day before Rosh Hashanah, the Dow Jones average saw its biggest drop ever, at 7 percent. Seven years later, on September 28, 2008 (which was also Elul 29), the day before Rosh Hashanah, the Dow fell 777 points, or another 7 percent! Do you see any connections here? Now, we are coming to the third and final shemittah since 1994, when Jupiter was hammered. Could the coming blood moons signal our third strike, and we will be out economically? We already see the signs of economic collapse coming, with America being so much in debt and our government in a comatose condition.

The Bible says that in the last days, knowledge will be increased (Dan. 12:4). This is not only secular knowledge but biblical insight as well. There will not be another tetrad happening on the biblical holidays in this century! This is the last warning. In the mouth of two or three witnesses let everything be established (2 Cor. 13:1). We have had the first two tetrad witnesses after Israel became a nation and then again when they recaptured Jerusalem. This is our third warning. I am not prophesying or predicting *what* will happen over the next two years, but if you look at the Scriptures alongside the patterns of history, we can definitely say two things. Based on what happened in 1948 and in 1967, there is a high probability of a major prophetic war that will involve Israel. At least a few major biblical wars are yet to come: the Isaiah 17 war, the Psalm 83 war, the Ezekiel 38 war, and the Zechariah 14 war. War often has a huge effect on the economy, which, based on the shemittah-year pattern, could be the other high-probability event.

To me, all these signs, coming together at one time, are potentially the culminating signals that God is closing this chapter of human history. This could be the final curtain call before the Great Tribulation mentioned in the Bible. God has always wanted to warn His people, and the rest of the world, before He intervenes. What better way to communicate to us than through the universal language of heavenly signs that speak to every tribe, tongue, and nation?

I conclude with a final thought. In Leviticus 23:3, Moses proclaimed: "Speak to the sons of Israel and say to them, The feasts of the LORD, which you *shall proclaim,*

holy convocations, even these are My appointed feasts."
According to *Strong's Concordance*, the Hebrew word for
"proclaim" gives the idea of accosting a person met: *calling
out* to or addressing by name *them that are bidden*, or to
invite, mention, publish, or read. This tells us that we are
responsible to "proclaim" the feasts of the Lord to others.
We are to bid them to come to the wedding! It's hard to
imagine, but there are people who do not want to come to
the wedding of the Messiah! Yet we are responsible to bid
them to come. We see this in the New Testament too:

> A certain king, which made a marriage for his son, . . .
> sent forth his servants to call *them that were bidden* to
> the wedding: and they would not come. Again, he sent
> forth other servants, saying, Tell them which are bidden,
> Behold, I have prepared my dinner: my oxen and my
> fatlings are killed, and all things are ready: come unto
> the marriage. (Matt. 22:2–4)

What is so unbelievable to me is what happens next:
"But *they made light of it*, and went their ways, one to his
farm, another to his merchandise" (v. 5). This concept is
restated in another way in the Gospel of Luke:

> Then said [Yeshua] unto him, A certain man made a
> great supper, and bade many: and sent his servant at
> supper time to say to them that were bidden, Come; for
> all things are now ready. And they all with one consent
> began to make excuse. The first said unto him, I have
> bought a piece of ground, and I must needs go and
> see it: I pray thee have me excused. And another said,
> I have bought five yoke of oxen, and I go to prove them:

I pray thee have me excused. And another said, I have married a wife, and therefore I cannot come. So that servant came, and shewed his lord these things. Then the master of the house being angry said to his servant, Go out quickly into the streets and lanes of the city, and bring in hither the poor, and the maimed, and the halt, and the blind. (Luke 14:16–21)

The Creator of the universe is calling you by name to come to the great supper! Will you come? And He asked those of us who are His servants to go and bid others to come to His Feast!

In the book of Daniel, Belshazzar could not read the "writing on the wall" (Dan. 5). Now that you understand the signs that are coming in the heavens and the timing of them on God's feast days, you can read the handwriting in the heavens! God is writing His message this time so the whole world can see it. And He is asking *you* to run with the interpretation of His message. But we must run with understanding. The Great Tribulation may be upon us and time is short, for the Day of the Lord is at hand!

The two main things to remember is (1) that the body of Messiah needs to get on God's calendar to understand the signs of the times, and (2) the reason we got off of it in the first place was because of the errant thinking behind replacement theology. This will be the critical issue in the last days, and here is why.

The book of Ruth is very prophetic. If you remember, Elimelech and Naomi were Jews living in Bethlehem. They had two sons: Mahlon and Chilion. There was no bread in Bethlehem, so they left their country. While they were exiled in a foreign land, for almost ten years, Naomi's husband died and her two sons married two Gentiles: Ruth and Orpah. These women represent the Gentiles who are grafted into the covenant of Israel by the God of Abraham, Isaac, and Jacob. So Ruth and Orpah, in one sense, also represent the "Church" that is grafted into the Branch.

When Naomi, the Jewess, heard there was bread again in Bethlehem, off she went, back to the land of Israel. This represents the restoration of Israel back to the land in 1948. But Naomi's two sons had also died by this time, so she told her two daughters-in-law not to follow her, but to instead go back to their people. Ruth cleaved to Naomi, but Orpah returned to her family and to her pagan gods. Naomi told Ruth: "Behold, thy sister in law is gone back unto her people, and unto her gods: return thou after thy sister in law. And Ruth said, Intreat me not to leave thee, or to return from following after thee: for whither thou goest, I will go; and where thou lodgest, I will lodge: thy people shall be my people, and thy God my God" (Ruth 1:15–16).

Ruth, whose name means "friend," returned to the land of Israel and worked the barley harvest, which is at Passover! Ruth 2:23 says, "She kept fast by the maidens of Boaz to glean unto the end of barley harvest and of wheat harvest; and dwelt with her mother in law." Ruth befriended the Jewish people; worked the harvest from Passover to Pentecost; ended up marrying the kinsman redeemer, Boaz; and brought forth the Messiah through King David!

What a story! So Ruth and Orpah represent the church in the final days. Orpah means "the back of the neck"; she turned her back on Israel and returned to her pagan lifestyle. The Babylonian Talmud says that Orpah begat Goliath, the *enemy* of Israel (Sotah 42b). So here we have the final epic battle lines being drawn in the church in these last days. The church will be divided between those who support Israel, work the harvest, and bring forth the Messiah, and those who turn their backs on Israel and form the one-world church. On one side will be those who love the God of Abraham, Isaac, and Jacob as David did, and this group will be small, as David was. On the other side will be the giant Goliath, the one-world church that hates God's people and wants to see them destroyed.

Where will you be standing on that final day? The test will be when you mention God's laws. When you say we should stand with the Jewish people, does an abnormal anger and hatred spew from their mouths? Do they allow the traditions of men to override the eternal truths of God's Word?

As you have been reading this book, you may be experiencing what I experienced. It is the same thing that hundreds of people have told me over the last twenty years that they experienced when studying Christianity's Jewish roots. When the eyes are opened the same statements are heard over and over: "I've been robbed!" or "Why wasn't I ever taught this?" Then they get angry at their pastors for not ever teaching this. I have to tell them they can't because people don't know what they don't know! If their pastors were never taught, how can you expect them to teach it? Some get mad or frustrated because they spent thousands of dollars on religious education only to find out they were given wrong or inaccurate information.

To them I say, come and join me! Invite your friends

and explore the Bible from a whole new fresh perspective! For me, this has been a complete cycle from the very beginning where I ran away from home as a child only to find out I was loved all along. Now I have returned home again to my Heavenly Father and truly find rest by aligning myself with His schedule.

BIBLIOGRAPHY

Braun, Moshe. *The Jewish Holy Days: Their Spiritual Significance.* Northvale, NJ: Jason Aronson Inc., 1996.

Brown, Michael. *Our Hands Are Stained With Blood, The Tragic Story of the "Church" and the Jewish People.* Shippensburg, PA: Destiny Image Publishers, Inc., 1990.

Chumney, Edward. *The Seven Festivals of the Messiah.* Shippensburg, PA: Destiny Image, 1994.

Fass, Y. Dr. *Creation's Heartbeat, The Bible's Entry Code in Genesis 1:1.* Laytonsville, MD: Otto RvF, 2009.

Glaser, Mitch and Zhava. *The Fall Feasts of Israel.* Chicago: Moody Press, 1987.

Gruber, Daniel. *The Separation of Church & Faith, Volume 1, Copernicus and the Jews.* (Hanover: Elijah Publishing, 2005).

Howard, Kevin, and Marvin Rosenthal. *The Feasts of the Lord, God's Prophetic Calendar from Calvary to the Kingdom.* Nashville: Thomas Nelson, Inc., 1997.

Koenig, William. *Eye to Eye, Facing the Consequences of Dividing Israel.* Springfield, MO: 21st Century Press, 2004.

Luton, Grant. *In His Own Words: Messianic Insights Into the Hebrew Alphabet.* Uniontown, OH: Beth Tikkun Publishing, 1998.

Neusner, Jacob, ed. "Bavli Tractate Sukkah, Chapter One, Folios 2A–20B." In *The Babylonian Talmud, A Translation and Commentary*, 113. Peabody, MA: Hendrickson Publishers, Inc., 2005.

Seekins, Frank. *Hebrew Word Pictures.* Scottsdale, AZ: Dr. Frank Seekins, 2012.

Ussher, James. *The Annals of the World.* Green Forest, AR: Master Books, 2003.

Whiston, William, ed. "The Wars of the Jews, Chapter 4." In *The Works of Josephus: New Updated Edition*, 742. Peabody, MA: Hendrickson Publishers, Inc., 1987.

RESOURCES

JEWISH CALENDAR

This site provides a complete history of the Jewish calendar as well as helpful charts so that you can be on God's calendar.

www.jewfaq.org/calendar.htm

HEBREW LANGUAGE STUDY

Danny Ben Gigi's Hebrew World is a great resource for learning Hebrew with Israel's spirit.

www.hebrewworld.com

LIVING WORD PICTURES

Dr. Frank T. Seekins teaches the transformational precepts found embedded in the ancient Hebrew language.

living-word-pictures.myshopify.com

EL SHADDAI MINISTRIES

A resource and teaching ministry to magnify the things Yeshua loves. Here you can access livestreaming events, handouts, newsletters, children's ministry resources, commentaries, and our *Feasts of the Lord* DVDs.

www.elshaddaiministries.us

NASA

This website shows when all the eclipses occur.

eclipse.gsfc.nasa.gov/LEcat5/LEcatalog.html

SUPERMOONS

Find out everything you need to know about supermoons.

www.timeanddate.com/astronomy/moon/super-full-moon.html

HEBREW CYPHER ART

Art encoded with Hebrew language.

www.hebrew-cypher-art.com

BREAKING NEWS

America's Independent News Network

www.wnd.com

INDEX

A

Aaron, divisions of the sons of, 114
abomination of desolation, 33
Adam, 36, 57, 83, 108, 136, 152
Against the Jews (Tertullian), 128
"Against the Jews" (Chrysostom), 133–34
Agape Force, 6, 7
Alhambra Decree, 134
America (the United States), 159
Americas, lunar eclipses in sky over the, 150
Annals of the World, The (Ussher), 31
annular solar eclipse, 146, 147
Antarctica, partial solar eclipse in the skies over, 155
Antichrist, 34, 49, 73, 92
Antiochus IV (Epiphanes), 33, 34
anti-Semitism, 85, 94, 133–37
appointed times, 48, 49, 54, 87, 89–90, 92, 123, 124
Arcturus, 43, 44
ark of the covenant, 98–99

Asia, lunar eclipses in sky over, 150
assimilation, 34
astronomy and astrology, contrasted, 39–40
Augustine of Hippo (saint), 134
Australia, lunar eclipses in sky over, 150
Av 9, 79, 125–26, 167

B

Babylonian Talmud, 31, 96, 135, 172
barley, 56, 57, 62, 99, 132, 171
biblical astronomy, 39–40, 42
blood moons
    definition, xvii
    NASA's term for four in a row, xvii
book of Revelation, 16, 27, 43, 62, 76, 85–86, 123, 160, 161
Boötes (constellation), 43, 44
Booths, Feast of. *See* Feast of Tabernacles
Braun, Moshe (rabbi), xv, 11

b'reisheet ("in the beginning"), 25–29

bride of Christ and bride of Song of Songs compared, 72–73

Bullinger, E. W., 40, 43, 145

C

calendar

basis for the Hebrew, 143

days and years of God's, 121–42

Gregorian, 123, 143

Jewish more complicated than Gregorian, 143

Mayan, 121

measuring the months in the Hebrew, 152

Muslim, 123

Carolingian Empire, dividing of, 148

Chanukah, 32, 33–34, 36, 45, 116

Chrislam, 34

Chrysostom, John (saint), 133–34

chuppah, 41, 81

Church, J. R., xii

church, one-world, 172

circumcision, 117–18

Columbus, Christopher, 134, 148

Constantine I, 128, 130–31

Coronation of the Messiah (HaMelech), 69, 82–84

Coronation Psalm, 83, 84

Council of Nicea (AD 325), 129

Creation, month of, 152

D

Daniel (the prophet), 49, 166–67

Daniel, book of, 27, 33, 49, 70–71, 72, 73, 76, 124, 166–67, 170

darkness,

physical, 29, 31, 53, 71, 78, 154

spiritual, 89, 111, 161

Day of Atonement (Yom Kippur), 62, 75, 94–95. *See also* Yom Kippur

Day of the Awakening Blast (Feast of Trumpets), 68, 72–74

Day of Blowing (Yom Teruah), 69

Day of Judgment (*aka* Yom HaDin), 69, 75, 77

Day of the Lord (*aka* time of Jacob's trouble), 29, 44, 68, 70–71, 77–80, 89, 154, 161, 170

connection to the shofars blown on Yom Teruah, 71

day of Pentecost, 59–60, 65, 171. *See also* Feast of Pentecost

Deuteronomy, 28, 35, 59, 73, 106, 107, 142, 167

Devarim, 167

Diaspora (the scattering of Jews in other nations), 74

Diotrephes (Greek pastor of 3 John), 127

Disengagement Plan (Sharon), 79

Dow Jones average, 167

E

earth, number of days it takes to revolve around the sun, 143 earthquakes, 30, 32, 70, 98

Easter, 130, 132

eclipses

on feast days around the time of the death of Christ (chart), 147

in the time frame around the destruction of the Temple (AD 70) (chart), 146

Elisabeth, 115, 116

El Shaddai Ministries, i, ii, vi, 12, 84, 121, 132

England, Jews kicked out of (Av 9, 1290), 126

enthronement ceremony of a Jewish king, four parts, 83

Europe

lunar eclipses in the skies over, 150

total solar eclipse in the skies over, 155

F

fall feasts, 61–63, 65–119. *See also* individual feasts by name

three that must be fulfilled at the Messiah's second coming, 161

fall harvest, 62–63

False Prophet, 92

Farah, Joseph, ix, x

feast, discussion of the Hebrew word (moed) for, 47–48, 50

feast days, as "dress rehearsals" for return of Christ for His bride, 41, 48, 50, 54, 57, 59, 60–61, 63–64, 84, 85, 90, 92, 95, 97

feast of the dedication, 32. *See* Chanukah

Feast of

Booths. *See* Feast of Tabernacles

Firstfruits, 56–57, 132

Harvest (*aka* Feast of Pentecost, Feast of Shavuot, Feast of Weeks), 48, 57–62, 99, 107, 115

Ingathering. *See* Feast of Tabernacles

Nations. *See* Feast of Tabernacles

Pentecost (*aka* Feast of Harvest, Feast of Shavuot, Feast of Weeks), 48, 57–62, 99, 107, 115 *See also* day of Pentecost

Shavuot (*aka* Feast of Harvest, Feast of Pentecost, Feast of Weeks), 48, 57–62, 99, 107, 115

Sukkot, 146. *See* Feast of Tabernacles

Tabernacles (*aka* Sukkot / Booths / Feast of Nations / Feast of Ingathering), xvii, 59, 62, 65, 74, 81, 95–96, 107–16, 143, 156, 158, 161

always during a full moon, 74

Jewish and Gregorian dates of (chart), 66

theme of, 65

what it celebrates (chart), 66

Trumpets (*aka* Rosh Hashanah, Yom Teruah), 62, 65, 66–72, 74, 75, 80–85, 92, 161

always during a new moon, 74

Jewish and Gregorian dates of (chart), 66

resurrection of the dead will happen at the, 69, 75

theme of, 65

what it celebrates (chart), 66

Unleavened Bread, 37, 55–56, 57, 59, 60, 62, 107, 143. *See also* Passover

always during a full moon, 74

Weeks (*aka* Feast of Harvest, Feast of Pentecost, Feast of Shavuot, *which see*), 57–60, 107

Yom Kippur. *See* Yom Kippur

feasts of the Lord

the Christian's responsibility to proclaim the, 169

misunderstanding of those who say they are done away with, 92–93

Ferdinand II (king), 134, 148

fig tree, 45

Firstfruits, Feast of, 56–57, 132

full moon, 74, 143, 155

odds of a, 155

super. *See* supermoon

G

Galatian paganism, 40, 93, 94

Gaza, 79–80, 126

God's

calendar days and years, 121–42

ultimate plan to dwell among His people, 108

Goliath, 172

grape harvest, 62–63, 99

Great Tribulation, 35, 45, 168, 170. *See also* time of Jacob's trouble

to start on the Feast of Trumpets, 71, 75

Gregorian calendar, 123, 143

Gregory XIII (pope), 123

H

Ha Kiddushin/Nesuin (Wedding of the Messiah), 69, 81–82

Hamas, 80

HaMelech (Coronation of the Messiah), 69, 82–84

Hanukkah. *See* Chanukah

harlot, the great, 90, 92

harvest

barley, 56, 57, 132, 171; and wheat, 62, 99, 171

feast of. *See* Feast of Harvest

grape, 62–63, 99

Harvest, Feast of. *See* Feast of Harvest

heavenly bodies used by God as signs, xviii, 20, 29–31, 35, 38, 39, 41, 44, 45, 47, 48, 49, 63, 65, 123, 124, 154, 160

Hebrew

aleph-bet (alphabet), 19–22, 29

calendar months, how they are measured, 152

language

as the "decoder ring" to God's hidden messages, 16

resurgence of, 17

word pictures in the, 19–29

Hebrew Word Pictures (Seekins), 19

Hidden Day (Yom HaKeseh), the, 69, 77–81

Hillel II, 131

Hitler, Adolf, 126, 137

Holocaust, 104, 162

holy days, xv, 93–94, 123

Hosea, book of, 45, 101–2

I

Iceland, total solar eclipse over, 115

Ingathering, Feast of. *See* Feast of Tabernacles

Irenaeus (bishop of Lyon), 128

Isabella I (queen), 134, 148

Isaiah (prophet), 25, 31

Isaiah (book of), xvi, 16, 28, 29, 70, 72, 80, 82, 96, 102, 109, 112, 118–19, 123, 129, 168

Islam, 34, 141

Israel, 12, 26, 28, 30, 31, 42, 44, 45, 46, 47, 51, 62, 66, 80, 96, 100, 102, 104, 107, 108, 112, 117, 123, 125, 126, 127, 129, 133, 139, 141, 154, 156, 165, 166, 168, 169, 171–72

becoming a nation again (1948), xvii, 45, 46, 127, 149, 158, 159, 168, 171

and occurrence of blood moons, xvii, 159, 168

represented by Naomi's return to Israel, 171

the church's erroneous claim to be the "true," 128

God's covenant never broken with, 103

Goliath (son of Orpah) the enemy of (Talmud), 172

the one tree, into which Christians are grafted, 103

partial spiritual blindness of, 103

J

Jerome (saint), 133

Jerusalem, xvi, 30, 32, 42, 44, 52, 58, 59, 61, 75, 82, 107–9, 110, 111, 113, 118, 119, 129, 154, 156, 158, 167

another word/name for (Zion), 23, 46

the Eternal Capital, 94

the final blood moon on the Feast of Tabernacles in 2015 will be seen from, 158

Israelites' recapture of (1967), xvii, 45, 46, 149, 168

Jesus. *See also* Yeshua

Europeanization of Jesus, 104

Hebrew name of, 23

a totally manufactured name, 104n

why Jews don't accept Him as the Messiah, 104–6

Jewish calendar, three heavenly events on which it is based, 143

Jewish Encyclopedia, 86

Jewish months and their equivalents on the Gregorian calendar (chart), 122

Jewish wedding ceremony, 41, 81
  in the Gospels, 81–82
  in Isaiah, coming of the Messiah
    based on, 82
  in Joel, 81
Joel, xvi, 29, 30, 43, 44, 45, 71, 81,
  123, 154
John (the apostle), 43, 97, 110, 113,
  123, 126, 127
John, gospel of, 22, 24, 27, 32, 81,
  111, 112, 113
John the Baptist, birth of, 113–16
Joseph (son of Jacob), 27, 54, 104,
  105
Josephus, Flavius, 33, 53, 97, 110
Jubilee years, 123
Jupiter, 93, 167
Justin (the) Martyr (saint), 128

K

keriah (Jewish mourning ritual of
  tearing of the clothes), 54
king, four parts to the enthronement
  ceremony of a Jewish, 83
knowledge, last-days increase in, 168

L

Laodicea, church of, 87
last days
  assimilation a sign of the, 34
  false peace during the, 22
  knowledge to increase in the, 168
"last trump," 67–68
Lebanon war (2007), 126

Leviticus, 26, 47–48, 51, 55, 56,
  57, 59, 66, 86, 92, 94, 96, 97,
  99–100, 107, 140, 141, 165,
  166, 168–69
lunar eclipse, 141, 144–46, 154
  odds of a, 155–56
  partial, 146, 147, 150
  penumbral, 146
  three types (according to NASA),
    144
  total, xvi, xvii, 147, 155
    four in a row in 2014 and
      2015, xvi
    number of occurrences from
      1999 BC to AD 3000, 144
    the only time one can
      scientifically occur, 143
Luther, Martin, 134–37

M

Maccabees, 33
Mark, gospel of, 51, 52, 91, 110,
  127
Martin V (pope), 148
Mary (mother of Christ), 115–16,
  118
Mayan calendar, 121
Mayans, 31
Messiah
  coronation of (HaMelech), 69,
    82–84
  second coming based on Jewish
    wedding ceremony in Isaiah, 82
  wedding of, 50, 69, 81–82, 169

millennial reign, 102

all nations will come to Jerusalem to learn the Torah during the, 119

months, Jewish and Gregorian (chart), 122

moon. *See also* blood moons

darkening of the, 29, 30, 35, 44, 45, 154

full. *See* full moon

God's faithful witness in the heavens, 42

Muslim calendar based on the, 123

new. *See* new moon

number of days it takes to revolve around the earth, 143

and sun used by God

as signs, xviii, 20, 29–31, 35, 38, 39, 41, 44, 45, 47, 48, 49, 63, 65, 123, 124, 154, 160

to determine feast days / days and years, 48, 122, 123

super full. *See* supermoon

in total eclipse, a bad omen for Israel, 31

turning into blood, xvi, 29, 30, 154

Moses, 20, 35, 47, 48, 66, 79, 95, 107, 110, 118, 128–29, 136, 138–41, 168–69

Mother of Harlots, 90, 172 (defined)

Mount of Olives, 32, 51, 108

mourning and fasting, 125

Muslim calendar, 123

N

NASA, xvi, xvii, 146, 150, 154, 157, 177

three kinds of eclipses as defined by, 144

Nations, Feast of. *See* Feast of Tabernacles

new moon, 74, 92, 93–94, 131, 143, 150, 152

ninth of Av, 79, 125–26, 167

Nisan 1, 141, 146, 147, 155

North Africa, total solar eclipse in the skies over, 155

northern Asia, total solar eclipse in the skies over, 155

Number in Scripture (Bullinger), 145

Numbers, book of, 55, 68, 69, 117, 128–29, 139, 140

O

odds

of a full moon, 155

of a lunar eclipse, 155–56

of a supermoon occurrence, 156

one-world church, 172

On the Jews and Their Lies (Luther), 134–37

Opening of the Books (Yom HaDin), 69, 75–77

Opening of the Gates (Yom HaDin), 69, 75–77

Order of Festivals (Talmud), 96n

Orion, 42–43

Orpah, representative of the apostate church, 171–72

P–Q

Pacific, lunar eclipses in sky over the, 150

Palestinians' rejection of "land for peace," 74

parable

of the fig tree, 45

of the talents (or five bags of gold), 91

of the tares (or weeds), 99

of the wedding banquet, 92, 169

of the wise and foolish virgins, 82, 87–88, 89

of the workers in the vineyard, 91

partial lunar eclipse, 144, 146, 147

partial solar eclipse, 155

Passover (*aka* Feast of Passover), xvii, 36, 37, 38, 48, 51–53, 55, 57, 62, 114, 115, 116, 128–32, 141, 143, 146, 147, 148, 155, 171. *See also* Feast of Unleavened Bread

date of occurrence each year, 132

Paul (the apostle), 40, 67–68, 89, 93–94, 132, 160–61, 165

Pentecost. *See* day of Pentecost; Feast of Pentecost

penumbral lunar eclipse, 144, 146

Pleiades, 42, 43

Pratney, Winkie, 7

prayers of the saints, 97–98

priests, courses of, 114

Prophecy in the News, xi–xii

prophet, biblical litmus test for determining a true, 34–35, 105–6

R

Ramadan, 123

rapture, 80, 160, 161, 163

Ravenhill, Leonard, 7

redemption, the theme of Yom Kippur, 65

rejoicing, the theme of the Feast of Tabernacles, 65

religious year, date of the beginning of the, 114, 146, 155

repentance, the theme of the Feast of Trumpets, 65

replacement theology, 12, 126, 170

restoration of all things, 16–17

resurrection

of Christ, 36, 56–58, 65

during the Feast of Firstfruits, 56–57, 62, 132

of the dead, 67–68, 69, 75, 80, 102

return of Christ. *See* Second Coming

Revelation, book of, 16, 27, 43, 62, 76, 85–86, 123, 160, 161

Rosh Hashanah, 28, 36, 62, 69, 143, 146–47, 155, 167

Ruth (biblical character)

and Orpah represent the Gentiles grafted into the covenant of Israel / the church, 171

Ruth, book of, 170, 171

S

sabbath days, 93–94

Sanhedrin, 131

saros cycle, 150, 151, 152

saros series, 150, 152, 154

science of the signs (in the heavens), 143–56

seasons, 38, 42, 47, 48, 50, 160, 161, 165

    fall feasts, 65–120

    meaning of the word, 89

    spring feasts, 47–64

Second Coming (return of Christ), 61, 63, 160

Seekins, Frank, 19

"Sermon against the Jews" (Augustine), 134

seven seals in Revelation, 160

seven sisters (stars), 42, 43

Sharon, Ariel, 79

Shavuot, festival of (*aka* Feast of Weeks, Feast of Harvest), 48, 58, 60, 62, 99, 115. *See also* Feast of Shavuot

Shema, 142

Shemini Atzeret, 117

shemittah year, 123, 165, 167, 168

Shoemaker-Levy 9 (comet), 167

shofar (trumpet), 67–68, 69, 71, 78, 82, 84–85

signs and signals, 15–46

    in heaven and earth, 29–46

    Hebrew aleph-bet as, 16–29

signs of the times, 89, 170

    the science of the, 143–56

signs of the times, requirement for God's people to understand the, 170

Six-Day War (1967), 159

solar eclipse, the only time one can scientifically occur, 143

Solomon, a type of the Antichrist, 73–74

Song of Songs, 72–73

South Africa, partial solar eclipse in the skies over, 155

Spain, Jews kicked out of (Av 9, 1492), 126

spiritual blindness. *See* veil, removing the

spring feasts, 47–64. *See also* individual feasts by name

    used as signs pointing to the death, burial, and resurrection of Yeshua, and the outpouring of the Holy Spirit at Pentecost, 65

Stearman, Gary, xii

Strong's Exhaustive Concordance of the Bible, 50, 66, 169

Sukkot, Feast of. *See* Feast of Sukkot; Feast of Tabernacles

sun

    darkening of the, 29, 30, 35, 44, 45, 154

    and moon used by God

        as signs, xviii, 20, 29–31, 35, 38, 39, 41, 44, 45, 47, 48, 49, 63, 65, 123, 124, 154, 160

        to determine feast days (and years), 48, 122, 123

        in total eclipse, a bad omen for the nations, 31

supermoon, 155, 156, 158

T

"tabernacles," the earth and our bodies only, 109

Tabernacles, Feast of. *See* Feast of Tabernacles

Talmud, 31, 96, 135, 172

Tanakh, number of references in Revelation, 16

Taurus (constellation), 43

Temple, 32, 33, 34, 53, 56, 57, 58, 59, 60, 61, 75, 95, 97, 100, 111, 112, 113, 114, 117

destruction, 108, 154

in 587 BC, 125, 126

in AD 70, 102, 126, 146: eclipses during the time frame around (chart), 146

four ominous events that took place forty years before the destruction of (in AD 70), as related by the Talmud, 96

heaven, everything on earth to be patterned after the temple in, 98

renting of the veil in the, 54

Yeshua to build the, 108

Tertullian, 128

teruah, meaning of, 69, 72

tetrad(s), 144

over the last two thousand years, chart of tetrads since the first century, 149

number of, 145

quick synopsis of, 147–49

NASA's definition, vii

in the past, vii

"thief in the night," Christ's return as, 85–89, 161

Thomas Aquinas, 137

time of Jacob's trouble (*aka* day of the Lord), 68, 70–71, 162. *See also* Feast of Trumpets

Torah, what God's encoded picture language tells us about, 24–25

total lunar eclipse, vi, vii, 141, 144–45, 147, 155

described, 144

four in a row in 2014 and 2015, vi

number of occurrences from 1999 BC to AD 3000, 144

the only time it can scientifically occur, 143

total solar eclipse, 141, 146, 147, 155

the only time it can occur, 31

Treaty of Verdun, 148

Tribulation. *See* Great Tribulation

Trumpets, Feast of. *See* Feast of Trumpets

U

Ulrich, Bob, i–ii

United Nations, 159

Upper Room, 60

Ussher, James, 31

V

Vayikra, 140–41

veil, removing the, 101–6

virgins, parable of the wise and foolish, 82, 87–88, 89

W–X

wars

  from 1894 to 1948 (World Wars I and II), 17, 154

  a sign of Yeshua's second coming, 32

  yet to come, 168

Wars of the Jews (Josephus), 97

Wedding of the Messiah, 50, 69, 81–82, 169

Weeks, Feast of. *See* Feast of Weeks

West Asia, lunar eclipses in the skies over, 150

Wilkerson, David, 7

Witness of the Stars (Bullinger), 40, 43

Women's Court, 110–11

World War I, 126, 154

World War II, 154

Y

year of Jubilee, 123

Yeshua. *See also* Messiah

  birth of (timing), 113, 116

  book of the Bible most quoted by, 106

  to build the temple of the Lord, 108

  circumcision of, 117–18

  death

    date of, 132, 147

    eclipses on feast days around the time of His death (chart), 147

    four ominous events that took place at the time of Yeshua's, 96

  meaning of the name, 23

was Jewish, 94

Yoma (Talmud), 96n

Yom HaDin (Day of Judgment/The Opening of the Books/Opening of the Gates), 75–77

Yom HaKeseh (the Hidden Day), 69, 77–81

Yom Kippur (Day of Atonement), 48, 62, 65, 75, 94–102, 105, 161

  connection between service in Leviticus and Revelation, 97–98, 99–100

  the day of removing the veil (that hides God from humanity), 101–2

  the day of vengeance on God's adversaries, 100

  Jewish and Gregorian dates of (chart), 66

  as Judgment Day, 99

  theme of, 65

  what it celebrates (chart), 66

Yom Teruah (Feast of Trumpets), 66, 69, 71, 78, 82–84. *See also* Feast of Trumpets

Z

Zacharias, 114, 115

Zechariah, 97, 108, 124–25, 168

Zephaniah, 17, 71, 77–79

Zion

  another name for Jerusalem, 23, 46

  built up, 46, 85

  example of Hebrew symbolism in the word, 23–24